ANTHROPOLOGY
FOR BEGINNERS®

ANTHROPOLOGY
FOR BEGINNERS®

BY MICAH J. FLECK
ILLUSTRATED BY LUCA F. CAREY

FOR BEGINNERS®

WEST SUSSEX LIBRARY SERVICE		
201985353		
Askews & Holts	07-Sep-2020	
301		

For Beginners LLC
30 Main Street, Suite 303
Danbury, CT 06810 USA
www.forbeginnersbooks.com

Copyright © 2020 Micah J. Fleck
Illustrations copyright © 2020 by Luca F. Carey

This book is sold subject to the condition that it shall not, by way of trade or otherwise, be lent, re-sold, hired out, or otherwise circulated without the publisher's prior consent in any form of binding or cover other than that in which it is published and without a similar condition being imposed on the subsequent purchaser.

All rights reserved. No part of this publication may be reproduced, stored in a retrieval system, or transmitted in any form or by any means, electronic, mechanical, photocopying, recording, or otherwise, without prior permission of the publisher.

A For Beginners® Documentary Comic Book
Copyright © 2020

Cataloging-in-Publication information is available from the Library of Congress.

ISBN # 978-1-939994-76-9 Trade

Manufactured in the United States of America

Typography by Dana Hayward

For Beginners® and Beginners Documentary Comic Books® are published by For Beginners LLC.

First Edition

10 9 8 7 6 5 4 3 2 1

To Morrison

ANTHROPOLOGY
FOR BEGINNERS®

Contents

Foreword	xiii
Introduction	1
1. What Is Anthropology? (And What It Is Not)	3
2. The Scientific Turn	23
3. Early Humans	45
4. Modern Insights	78
5. Four Subfields, A Unique Advantage	120
6. Future Frontiers	127
Glossary	133
Further Reading	137
About the Author	139
About the Illustrator	139

FOREWORD
by John L. Jackson, Jr.

Anthropology shouldn't just be for anthropologists. Not even close.

At my most generous, I might characterize this seemingly quirky little discipline as a particularly empathic way of living life in a diverse world, a way of being that places a premium on learning all we can through close attention to what we observe people doing and saying, both now and in the past: what they eat and where they live, how they bury their dead and protect their families, who they love and who they hate. This is all undeniably juicy fodder for what Muriel Dimen in the 1970s called "the anthropological imagination." But how should we imagine anthropology?

I like to tell my students that anthropology is both the most hubris-filled and humble academic discipline on the planet.

Its hubris comes from the fact that card-carrying anthropologists are situated within and across the humanities, the social sciences and the natural sciences, those three major buckets distinguishing and comprising all academic fields in higher education. No other discipline can boast that kind of wide-ranging reach—not philosophy, not psychology, not even physics.

Anthropologists try to determine precisely what makes human beings humans. What makes us similar to—and different from—any other sentient creature? One answer to that question is simple: every single thing you can think of, which is why self-proclaimed anthropologists consider anything fair game for study, from primate mating rituals in the Amazon to scientific research practices among those working on the Higgs Boson in Geneva. Wherever and whenever you find humans doing and saying things, you have discovered data ripe for anthropological investigation. That realization also helps to explain what I might describe as anthropology's humility.

At its core, anthropologists claim that any human being, living or dead, is a powerful ambassador for the social universe they inhabit. They can be a princess or a pauper, an opera singer or a hip-hop emcee. If we really pay attention to what people tell us about the worlds they come from, either through texts found in contemporary archives or as organic remains left in the ground from thousands of years ago, we will learn something valuable about the human condition. In some ways, the more seemingly trivial the subject, the more profoundly its thoughtful analysis can help us rethink fundamental questions about human life.

We used to debate the difference between nature and nurture in determining human potential. Is biology destiny, or does our social environment play a deciding role in shaping people's lives and life chances? Anthropologists have always been in the middle of such academic disputes, and they continue to operate at the intersection of biology and culture, some making a case for the biological proclivities we share with other species, others arguing that most popular understandings of biology are just cultural ideas dressed up to look and feel like genetic mandates. The history of anthropology as a so-called "race science" is all about such machinations. This book helps to make sense of those debates, both by unpacking the four traditional subfields of American anthropology and by showing how normative assumptions about humanity have changed in fascinating and fundamental ways over time.

It seems particularly appropriate to me that this short primer on the field starts with a metaphor straight out of science fiction: aliens landing on earth from another galaxy. We tend to think of anthropologists as people who traffic in the past, in bygone eras, but as our field continues to grow and evolve, as it seeks to stay relevant and insightful, it asks key questions not just about where we've been but about what kind of future we might envision and create. The specific features of this would-be future aren't a foregone conclusion. Far from it. And anthropologists have increasingly come to grips with the central role of force and power in the shaping of all social communities, even as traditional anthropological renditions of "primitive" social life sometimes positioned and pretended modern power-plays (such as colonialism and imperialism) out of ethnographic view.

One current debate within the field boils down to different takes on how political the work of anthropologists can/should be. Is it enough for anthropologists to simply be curious, to want to know something for the sake of knowing it, or must they always emphasize the ways in which social lives are parsed into the relatively powerless and powerful? And what kind of power does the anthropologist wield? This brief overview helps to start the reader on a journey towards answering those questions, and it covers interesting anthropological arguments in ways that are worth considering whether or not one ever intends to become a professional anthropologist—though the latter can be pretty cool, too.

John L. Jackson, Jr. is Richard Perry University Professor of Anthropology and Communication as well as Walter H. Annenberg Dean of the Annenberg School for Communication at the University of Pennsylvania. In addition to being an anthropologist, and a filmmaker, he is also author of several books, including Thin Description: Ethnography and the African Hebrews of Jerusalem.

Introduction

IMAGINE YOU'RE AN ALIEN FROM OUTER SPACE—YOU'VE been exploring the cosmos, and most recently landed on planet Earth. You are fascinated by the planet's organic inhabitants, especially the most intellectually divergent of all the primates: Homo sapiens. You want to know as much about them as possible in your limited time visiting Earth, including by what means these Homo sapiens (who call themselves "humans") came to physically be, and how and why they have built their incredibly diverse cultures and languages. If only there were a hyper-focused field of inquiry that could cover all of these questions and serve as a singular resource of relevant data all about humans' biology, cultures, and societies . . .

As it turns out, there *is* a concentrated field of study of this nature. It is called anthropology, and it is one of the richest scientific fields ever devised. But what *is* it, exactly? It is easy to cite its literal definition, "the study of people," and completely miss out on what specific expertise anthropology has to offer, and what tools it has given its very subject, us, as a means of uncovering the mysteries of our species— through space and time.

Over the centuries, the field of anthropology has itself gone through key transformations that have helped mold it into the empirical and testable science that it is today. As a result, the general population's understanding of what anthropology even involves or what an anthropologist herself does can vary widely. This volume you now hold in your hands intends to contribute in its own small way toward correcting that confusion. Is anthropology, for instance, just a humanities field, or does it follow the scientific method like the other natural

I

sciences? Is an anthropologist someone who digs around in the dirt to uncover old artifacts from long-dead civilizations, or someone who instead examines the living, breathing cultures of the here and now? What is the difference between anthropology and sociology?

The answers to these questions are more nuanced than one might realize, but they are also very straightforward. The key is to understand that anthropology itself is a very interdisciplinary field with several different approaches to understanding society and the people who live within it. While many academic fields reap seemingly clashing perspectives between the social and life sciences, between academic perspectives and everyday life, anthropology is unique in its ability to not only build the bridges between these worlds, but to reside within and between them with empirical certainty and a concern for the well-being and understanding of all humans—past, present, and future. To understand how, we must start at the beginning . . .

✦ 1 ✦
What Is Anthropology?
(And What It Is Not)

IN THE MOST STRAIGHTFORWARD OF TERMS, ANTHRO-pology is the scientific study of human kind through space and time. More specifically, it is a field of inquiry that uses multiple methods for gathering information about human beings and the societies we build—in the past, and in the present. To do this, anthropologists call on research techniques pulled from both the hard sciences and the social sciences whenever the inquiry in question demands one approach or the other.

For instance, when anthropologists need to learn more about present-day societies that have yet to be well-documented, field researchers known as **ethnographers** are sent to live amongst the citizens of the society in question and keep meticulous record of how the society works. In this example, anthropologists are using both sociological methods and more scientifically-minded data gathering and observation—often for months and even years at a time—before reaching conclusions about the how and why behind the function of said culture.

On the other hand, if the people and places being studied have been gone for centuries, anthropologists will utilize other methods completely, such as archaeology and radiocarbon dating, to dig up and then determine the age of past artifacts, bones, and fossils these long-gone societies left behind.

ANTHROPOLOGY FOR BEGINNERS

In studying both past and present cultures, anthropologists must also be able to learn other languages so they can either communicate with the living or read the historical records of the dead. And in determining the causes for certain human behaviors, anthropologists investigate potential origins in both cultural and biological arenas.

What Is Anthropology? (And What It Is Not)

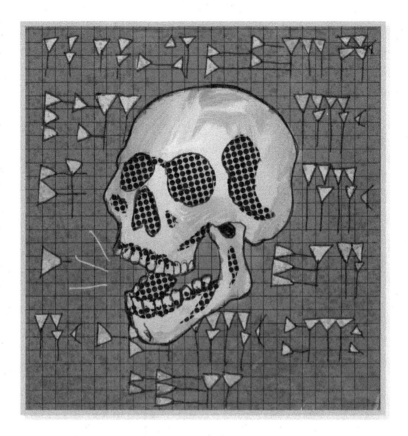

These and other examples illustrate just how interdisciplinary the field of anthropology is, and why it is necessarily so. But to really grasp the full picture of anthropology as a rich science with multiple applications, we need to dig deeper into and clearly define the four major subfields of anthropology: **archaeology, linguistics, sociocultural anthropology**, and **biological anthropology**.

The Four Subfields of Anthropology

ARCHAEOLOGY: This field of study was originally all there was to scientific anthropology, and it predates the use of the term "anthropology" in academic circles. Stemming from an even earlier tradition of collecting material histories known as **antiquarianism**, archaeology found its empirical methodology during the Enlightenment in seventeenth century Europe. These methods included meticulous excavation tactics that were designed to not disrupt the riches awaiting discovery underground.

These developments meant that for the first time, material history could be completely preserved and utilized for more academic inquiry into humanity's past. Taking this into account, it is very reasonable to

What Is Anthropology? (And What It Is Not)

take the position that archaeologists were the first true anthropologists.

Today, archaeology is largely considered to be one of the four main subdisciplines of modern anthropology, with an even more interconnected approach, dubbed "processual archaeology," bringing in the other subfields such as linguistic and cultural anthropology to paint a more holistic picture of excavational findings.

LINGUISTIC ANTHROPOLOGY: At the crossroads between basic linguistics and the study of language's influence on humanity resides linguistic anthropology. Though it is still technically correct to call this subfield simply "linguistics," it should be noted that linguists and linguistic anthropologists are not always investigating the same questions. Traditional linguistics dealt with more structural questions that were innately present in language itself, but the field's merging with anthropology started to take place when linguists began to draw connections between language itself and cultural perception and interaction. From then on, language's integral relation to human society became a constant concern for linguistic researchers.

The world of linguistics was rocked yet again in the 1950s when it was discovered that humans seem to possess an innate capacity to understand structured language—independently of prior schooling on the matter. This has come to be known as universal grammar, and the latest studies into its origins have led linguistic anthropologists to combine their research with that of biological anthropologists in hopes that an evolutionary cause can be pinpointed. In this way, linguistic anthropology is itself just as interdisciplinary as the broader field of anthropology as a whole.

ANTHROPOLOGY FOR BEGINNERS

SOCIOCULTURAL ANTHROPOLOGY: It is a little harder to pin down the origin point for this particular subfield; the first self-described anthropologists in the nineteenth century *were* technically cultural anthropologists, however, most of their methodologies and conclusions have long-since been debunked as unscientific. As such, we will define sociocultural anthropology as it exists in its present form, having been "rebooted" in a sense at the dawn of the twentieth century as needing to rely heavily on work done by field researchers (those aforementioned ethnographers) and/or abide by scientific standards of inquiry.

What Is Anthropology? (And What It Is Not)

In a nutshell, modern sociocultural anthropologists are primarily concerned with the ways in which human beings build and interact with their cultural surroundings, and conversely, how said surroundings go on to inform human behavior. This means that if you are a cultural anthropologist, you could take on research dealing with non-Western *and* Western societies, cultures of the past *or* present, base your work on long-term participant observation in the field, or through an academic analysis of existing data, and so on. You are limited only by your imagination and the empirical nature of your research—aside from that, the sky is the limit regarding what topics, regions, and peoples you may choose to discover.

Many other fields of inquiry are pulled from by cultural anthropologists depending on the research at hand, including psychology, sociology, primatology, history, economics, and of course, the other subfields of anthropology. Through sociocultural anthropology we have discovered deeper truths about cultural difference and sameness, socially constructed concepts such as race and gender, the relative nature of cultural comparison, the benefits of cultural and intellectual diversity, and more. All of this makes sociocultural anthropology arguably the richest discipline within an already rich research field.

BIOLOGICAL ANTHROPOLOGY: The other contender for richest subdiscipline, biological anthropology's primary concern is the process of human evolution. It pulls from paleontology, primatology, evolutionary biology, genetics, medical science, and anatomy, and puts into practice techniques such as radiocarbon dating, new computer scanning technology, site excavation, and others as it strives to better understand the physical side of human-centric study. But not just how basic anatomy evolved, but also how certain behavioral trends came about that can be observed both within cultures and individual interactions. Customs such as bowing as a sign of reverence in religious traditions, for instance, seem to transcend geography, and there are both evolutionary and cultural research avenues one can take to understand where such physical motions came from and why humans seemed predisposed to adopt them.

Biological anthropologists have also paved the way toward understanding why certain regions' inhabitants develop certain medical disorders more frequently than others, or whether or not a person's **phenotype** (the trait that shows) is genetically significant.

What Is Anthropology? (And What It Is Not)

As we can see, these specialized disciplines within anthropology have their own focuses and expertise, and bring their unique and useful answers to the broader human observation, all while relying on each other to inform the context and fill in the gaps of certain findings along the way. Taken separately, no individual specialization in anthropology would be nearly as useful in understanding the complexities of the human condition as they are when brought together. This makes anthropology a truly special field of study that is uniquely equipped to best understand ourselves and the cultures we build on both the social and biological frontiers.

ANTHROPOLOGY FOR BEGINNERS

> **Hey, buddy! That's a lot of information!**

While it is important to understand that anthropology has multiple areas of focus, the point of this knowledge is to simply inform, not to overwhelm. Remembering the specific strengths and hyper-detailed focuses of each field of anthropology will not be required to enjoy the rest of this volume; what *will* be important is that you simply remember that anthropology takes a holistic approach to its topics of interest. That way, the multi-layered nature of many of anthropology's key discoveries will make more sense than it might without such context.

Is This a Science or a Humanities Field?

There is still some debate in certain circles about whether or not anthropology can be called a science, considering the fact that two of the four subdisciplines are not, strictly speaking, scientific in nature. While it is true that the natural sciences are not front and center in linguistic and cultural anthropology, it also cannot be ignored that those fields still base their research and conclusions on scientifically established foundations. Ever since anthropology's turn toward empirical accuracy and scientific bases in the early twentieth century, all of its subfields have been informed by scientific truths—cultural and linguistic anthropology included.

After all, it is on a genetic basis that modern cultural anthropologists can safely state that concepts such as race are in fact culturally defined and not biologically measurable; and it is only because of advancements in cognitive science that many linguistic anthropologists can now argue in favor of language being a unique product of human

What Is Anthropology? (And What It Is Not)

biology, and not just a learned attribute that we happened to master before any other animal.

Therefore, while it is true that anthropology as a whole is indeed a science, it is equally correct to say that not every individual anthropologist is necessarily a scientist. But every type of anthropologist who is active in the field still plays an equally important role in bringing forth empirical truths about humanity in all its aspects.

Okay, But What About Sociology?

Many people over the years have often conflated or interchanged sociology with anthropology in everyday conversation. And it is understandable to see why, since both fields spend a lot of time investigating human societies through an academic lens. However, there are two major differences between the two fields:

1) **THE PRIMARY FOCUS.** Whereas sociology is mainly concerned with studying societies at large and their functionality (from "above"), anthropology digs deeper and approaches the study of society by starting with the human elements (from "within"). From there, anthropologists find the cultural and/or biological relevance for a given society's characteristics. Sociology also tends to be more localized in its focus while many anthropologists seek out cultures other than their own as a means of painting a fuller picture of humanity outside the Western-influenced world.

2) **THE RANGE OF EXPERTISE.** Anthropology is both multidisciplinary and interdisciplinary to a very high degree. What this means is that anthropology is far better equipped to take on the bigger questions about human kind than sociology, especially once the questions lead us outside the confines of social science and into nature itself.

Different; not better or worse. This is a core value of anthropology when studying and comparing different cultures and people. This same principle applies when comparing sociology to anthropology on their academic merits. Both fields have important parts to play, and there is certainly overlap between them whenever anthropologists build upon sociological data, but sociologists attempt to map specific elements of society while anthropologists attempt to understand humanity. It's just different approaches, and both are equally valid for the particular questions each field is trying to answer.

What Is Anthropology? (And What It Is Not)

> **SAPIEN SIDELINE: ORIGINS OF A WORD**
> The word "anthropology" actually traces much further back than its first use as a title for an academic field—all the way back to the ancient Greeks! Although, in those days the term would have translated to something like, "to enjoy personal conversation." Hardly the same meaning. Still, the Classical Greek words it is derived from, *anthrōpos*, meaning "human," and *logia*, meaning "study," hinted at the way the term would come to be used in the present-day.

Why All This Confusion?

Like many sciences, anthropology has not always had the best track record of being made easy to understand in mainstream presentations. Often, it is assumed that the audience already has a general grasp of what anthropology is—much in the same way most people know that astronomy deals with planets and neuroscience deals with the brain. The difference here is that anthropology itself has gone through some significant changes in content and approach, and its older variation unfortunately lingers in the broader social perception.

But what exactly changed? What did anthropology look like at its outset?

The Early Days of Anthropology

To be sure, even anthropologists themselves had trouble pinning down precisely what their field entailed at the very beginning. The earliest officially recognized anthropologists were little more than glorified explorers with journals by today's standards. In said journals, they kept record of their observations of other cultures and people they encountered on their travels. The first mainstream uses of the label "anthropologist" began cropping up in the late eighteenth and early

ANTHROPOLOGY FOR BEGINNERS

nineteenth centuries in British academic circles, and while it was often considered a "science" even then, the criteria to which anthropologists held themselves as they did their research was not at all in line with what we understand the scientific method to entail today.

What resulted from these initially loose requirements for anthropology research was a very imprecise method for documenting other

What Is Anthropology? (And What It Is Not)

cultures and people outside the Western world. Often, the earliest anthropologists would simply judge the merits of a different culture by viewing it through their own culturally informed perspective. Have you ever watched a foreign language film and suddenly been surprised (or even horrified!) by a choice of food or recreational practice? Of course, in the depicted culture, such things are completely normal, but to you, perhaps, it all appears highly unusual. This does not mean that the other culture's ways (called **mores**) are inherently worse than your own, but it does mean that you might not know what to make of them at first sight. This is the unfortunate position many of the early anthropologists found themselves in, and as a result, they would make knee-jerk assumptions about the cultural and moral values of other people whose own mores were different from those who observed them. This needlessly narrow perspective of other cultural conventions is something present-day anthropologists now call **ethnocentrism**, and it went on to nearly tarnish anthropology's reputation as a valuable field forever.

Around the time that Charles Darwin's theory of evolution by natural selection was taking the academic world by storm, there were certain wings of researchers who capitalized on its popularity and incorrectly applied scientific-sounding jargon to unscientific concepts. Darwin's new theory provided terminologies and descriptions for these bad actors to cannibalize and inject into their own vocabulary, even when they were presenting ideas completely unrelated to what Darwin's theory actually stated. What came from this was an extremely muddled vision of what was actually known about human biology at the time, misconstruing human diversity as snapshots of different evolutionary stages, and therefore conflating the concepts of "evolution" and "progress."

This fundamental misunderstanding of evolution, combined with the ethnocentric cultural observations of the aforementioned early anthropologists, gave birth to a concept known as social Darwinism.

ANTHROPOLOGY FOR BEGINNERS

The tagline for this social outlook, in which only the "superior" people survive, was "survival of the fittest," and there is a good chance that you have heard that phrase repeated even in the present-day. The ironic thing about this is that Darwin himself did not coin that phrase;

sociologist Herbert Spencer did in 1864. In fact, it was largely Spencer's insistence that the theory of natural selection could be applied to society and culture that helped solidify social Darwinism as a legitimized approach for studying human beings in the first place. Had history gone a slightly different way, perhaps we would have come to know this perspective as "Spencerism" and would have therefore discarded its claims long ago. Unfortunately for anthropology, the association with Darwin stuck, and as a result, the misconception has survived to this day that societies' values are objective rather than relative, and that human evolution is a march of progress rather than a result of circumstantial adaptation.

EVOLUTION IS NOT A LADDER

While this is not a biology textbook, a basic level of understanding for how evolution works is still helpful for those who might wonder how we know that human evolution is merely the process of adaptive change over time and not a forward march into moral superiority and prosperity. To achieve that, we are going to briefly follow Charles Darwin through his own journey of understanding regarding this process.

Charles Darwin's discovery and ultimate explanation of natural selection is documented most plainly across three of his books: *The Voyage of the Beagle* (1839), *On the Origin of Species* (1859), and *The Descent of Man* (1871). In *Voyage*, Darwin's discoveries on the Galapagos Islands are documented—key among them, a group of incredibly diverse-looking birds that Darwin at first suspects are all brand new exotic species. Upon further investigation, however, Darwin is shocked to find out that every single one of the bird types belong to the same species: the finch. The conclusion that Darwin ultimately comes to in subsequent revisions of the text is that this was a case of natural selection occurring within a very confined space with multiple environmental differences, and therefore "one species had been taken and modified for different ends," taking special note of the wildly diverse beak structures present among these finches depending on which island they inhabited.

On the Origin of Species goes further into detail regarding the process of natural selection. In short, evolution is change over time, and natural selection is the mechanism through which said change takes place. This occurs through the process of giving birth to offspring whose unique traits serve as more advantageous to surviving in one's immediate surroundings. Taking Darwin's finches as an example: if a baby bird is born with a small beak on an island where smaller nuts are less plentiful, then it is likely that that bird will not live as long or spawn as many children as needed to keep her bloodline alive for more than a couple of generations. However, if a bird is born on that same island with a larger beak that is capable of cracking open *all* sizes of nuts, then that bird is far more likely to have access to more food, live a longer, healthier life, pass on her particular traits to her own children, who will then benefit from *their* advantages, spawn their own children, and so on. Play this game for a million years, and the particular genetic modification that gives finches larger beaks will simply win the game of chance enough times to outnumber and ultimately overtake the smaller-beaked gene. The end result is a different finch for every island, each adapted for survival in that particular region.

The Descent of Man took everything Darwin had learned up to that point about natural selection and finally applied it specifically to human beings. Why is human diversity not a marker of "superior" or "inferior" people or societies? The same reason why Darwin's finches are not evidence of a linear progression of the finch. Each type of finch Darwin observed on the Galapagos Islands was more or less at the same "stage" of evolution as its brethren, but specific population bottlenecks at different environmental points around the islands had made necessary very different adaptive traits to win out in each region.

The result of this process of slow adaptive change through generations was the "one species" Darwin mused about in *Voyage* that had adapted only at the surface level (i.e. in the *phenotype*, or the trait that shows) for the purposes of merely surviving based on nothing but pure chance of location and climate. Human beings have evolved in much the same way, and we too are one species at the same stage of evolution in every region we inhabit. Our cultures, therefore, are the results of our interactions with our immediate surroundings, and are *not* predetermined by some linear forward progression from "primitive" to "advanced" like many of the early anthropologists and social Darwinists claimed. And while Darwin took the then-current anthropological literature into account when he wrote *Descent*, his ultimate conclusion was that all human beings evolved from a "single stock," and that once evolution became understood by everyone, the argument between his position and the social Darwinists' would "die a silent and unobserved death."

What we can bring with us from this bit of history is the knowledge that fallible, biased human beings are behind every bit of academic research that has ever been undertaken—whether it be in the sciences or the humanities. And without a firm bedrock of consistently self-correcting methodology, the conclusions from said research will always run the risk of housing that same bias. This is why, when studying humanity holistically, it was always important for anthropologists to ground their own research in the scientific method. But for a long time, this remained not the case. Until, that is, the turn of the century, and the arrival in America of a physicist who saw the potential of anthropology upon adhering it to the same testable, empirical principles of his own field. As we turn to the next chapter, it is time we met Franz Boas, the father of modern anthropology.

✦ 2 ✦

The Scientific Turn

IN 1896, A SCHOLAR FROM GERMANY INTERESTED IN COMbining anthropological inquiry with empirical scientific practices joined the faculty at Columbia University in New York City and began what became a revolution in anthropological thought and methodology. A physicist by training, this scholar recognized that by applying **the scientific method** to the study of human culture, much of the social Darwinist claims still popular in the field at the time were immediately discredited due to their own lack of grounding in falsifiable, observable evidence. This scholar's name was Franz Boas, and his PhD dissertation, though not directly related to anthropology, was about the color of water and how universal truths accounted for the phenomenon despite the seemingly subjective nature of what the color of water can appear to be from different perspectives and under different conditions. This ability to distinguish between empirical truth and subjective interpretations of said truth lent itself well to tackling the problem of ethnocentrism that was rampant in early anthropological literature.

So, over the course of his forty-year stay at Columbia, Dr. Boas worked toward formulating a new, scientifically grounded approach to anthropology, rejecting the prior notions of superior vs. inferior cultures, as well as the **unilinear evolutionism** of the so-called "march of progress" mentality regarding different cultures supposedly existing in different stages along a predetermined timeline of human development. While its title may itself come across as perpetuating these notions, Boas's 1911 book *The Mind of the Primitive Man* actually went a long way toward articulating arguments *against* the concept of the white "race" being superior to other "races" (and as we will see later through our discussion of evolutionary anthropology's greatest discoveries, the concept of "race" itself within humanity is biologically unsound). In fact, Boas made very clear in his writings that many nations of various ethnic groups were collectively responsible for building and perpetuating human civilization as a whole, and that there is no biological basis for cultural superiority at all.

But, how did Boas know this beyond a doubt? How does empirical reading of evidence come into play on this front? Well, that can be explained through a brief summary and understanding of the scientific method, which we will explore now!

THE SCIENTIFIC METHOD

Up until the seventeenth century, scientists were part of a long tradition of broader thinkers called natural philosophers who would make guesses about phenomena they observed happening in the world around them through use of their native senses. If you could see something with your own eyes, you could hypothesize the how and why behind said observation. Beyond that, you could wonder and philosophize, but your means of proving or disproving these notions as factual were very slim.

Those limitations began to lift with the invention of new technology and the serious implementation of mathematics into the study of stargazing (which we now call astronomy). With the invention of the first telescope came the ability to read light patterns as a means of determining speeds, distances, and trajectories of the various heavenly bodies that were too far away to observe in this manner with the naked eye. One particular astronomer from Iraq, known as Alhazen, was among the first natural philosophers to propose over a thousand years ago that formulating specific questions about nature, and then testing those questions against observed phenomena, was the key approach for natural philosophers to aspire to. Once the first telescope was invented, that same field had legitimate means to begin putting that principle into practice, and Galileo revived and endorsed Alhazen's notions as he went on to perform his own revolutionary work that would go on to confirm the helio-centric view of the solar system and provide important groundwork for future scientists of various fields to build upon in their own observational research.

This observational research now adheres to what is widely known as the scientific method. Its most recent form took shape at the turn of the twentieth century (around the same time Franz Boas was reinventing anthropology), and it follows the hypothetico-deductive model, which is structured into four steps as follows:

1) If prior experience in a given area of inquiry has already formed a foundation, gather what data you can from that existing scholarship and try to make sense of the observed phenomena.

2) If that fails, or if not enough data is already gathered for the particular inquiry at hand, then begin making educated guesses about the observed phenomena in order to build a **hypothesis**.

3) Then, follow the conditions of this hypothesis to their logical conclusions and make predictions of what further phenomena will be observed if the hypothesis is true.

4) If those predictions fail and different results arise through this further observation, then the hypothesis is wrong and a new one must be formulated. If, however, the results match the prediction, then further tests are done and more observation takes place in an attempt to still disprove the hypothesis. Once enough of these tests continue to be passed and the predictions continue to be correct, the hypothesis graduates to the level of **scientific theory** and is therefore taken as the current gold standard of explanation for the phenomena in question—until perhaps an even more resilient theory one day comes along.

In the case of the theory of evolution, for instance, it was once a hypothesis whose predictions went on to be proven beyond a doubt in related fields such as genetics and biology, which therefore made it one of the most resilient and trustworthy theories in all of science.

ANTHROPOLOGY FOR BEGINNERS

For Franz Boas, his desire to apply this sort of empirical, tested approach to the explanations for human diversity meant that without a similarly rigorous background, social Darwinism had no place in the discussion. Instead, Boas and his colleagues at the emergent anthropology department at Columbia proposed a different way of approaching the study of human diversity: **cultural relativism**. Through this lens, all humans are viewed as they are scientifically proven to be: equally evolved people who simply live in different regions of the world due to migration and population bottlenecking over the past 100,000 years, and whose cultural customs and norms contain unique characteristics that are informed by region, climate, and prior cultural interactions. In other words, *circumstance* makes a culture into what it is, and not biology.

One of many ways Boas and crew set about proving this fact was through empiricism (of course). When comparing so-called "primitive" cultures from different regions to one another, it became obvious that there were no consistent trends that could be identified across all of them. For instance, "sophistication" became a very relative concept from region to region and culture to culture, with some cultures in one region seemingly lacking so-called sophistication in technology or material wealth, but having incredibly sophisticated and complex social structures (such is the case with the Australian Aboriginals); on the other hand, equally "primitive" cultures in another region have less complexity in these social areas, but have incredibly high artisan and artist sophistication (this was found to be true in the Indians of California, for instance).

Such lack of uniformity in this so-called linear progression from primitive to sophisticated could not be explained through an unscientific application of natural selection principles onto cultural development; however, it *could* be explained through a more evidence-based approach to data gathering that took each unique culture's surrounding contexts into account. Instead of applying a blanket, uniform concept of point-A to point-B development to every culture, what needed to be done instead, contended the empirical anthropologists, was a process of direct observation of each culture from within, utilizing the same language and resources, and residing in the same region as the people being studied. This practice has come to be known as **ethnography**, and through it, ethnocentrism is directly combatted and discouraged, while a deeper, more empirical understanding of the given region and its people is developed.

Ethnography as an Empirical Grounding for Cultural Study

The process of ethnography is fascinating because it requires the anthropologist conducting the research to make a distinction between *moral* relativism and *cultural* relativism. For the individual researcher (who is rightly called an ethnographer), certain traditions may be encountered that are deemed morally wrong, and in many of those cases, depending on how one views the concept of universal morality, that opinion might be completely valid. But to be a successful ethnographer, the anthropologist must put on his or her ethnographer cap and nonetheless strive to *understand*, not necessarily condone, the practice or tradition being observed from a contextual perspective.

This approach ensures the most empirical, unbiased gathering of data possible during the anthropologist's time living among the people in question. In addition, any other cultural norms as informed by the culture of the ethnographer's own society are also rejected as

The Scientific Turn

base level assumptions regarding how another society should work, or how humans "naturally" behave. Even when outside the question of morality, these Western cultural norms can taint an anthropologist's approach to gathering data about another society that is different from her own. This is in many cases what caused the concept of the "savage" and the "primitive man" to endure far longer than the evidence accounted for: researchers were still looking at other societies through an ethnocentric, Western lens. The new empirical, participatory approach found in ethnography finally provided a means of dodging these pitfalls and getting a more contextually relevant reading of a given society's daily reality.

ANTHROPOLOGY FOR BEGINNERS

Of course, if something truly detrimental and/or horrific occurs such as a genocide, murder, or other act forced upon an involuntary participant or victim, that is an obvious exception to the general rule of thumb of not disrupting a different society's cultural norms for the sake of science. No moral anthropologist is going to take the position that such things are "okay" simply because they are occurring in another society. And this is why it is again important to distinguish between moral relativism and cultural relativism: sometimes, the former position is untenable while the latter can still be in play. In other words, one can still respect the fundamental cultural differences between one's own culture and the one being observed while simultaneously abhorring and even actively fighting against human atrocities being committed by that same society. After all, the evil acts individual people commit are themselves not reflections of every citizen of a given country or region. This is true of all cultures, both familiar and mysterious.

Universal Benefits of Ethnographic Fieldwork

One of the coolest realizations that studying each culture on its own terms through ethnographic research has brought humanity as a whole is the twofold discovery that humanity itself is both uniform *and* diverse. What we can break this down to is the fact that *because* we are all so different, that is what makes us ironically the same. Each human culture has common threads somewhere along the way, most likely due to the fact that all of humanity originated in the same region (Africa), and then migrated to other continents over our roughly two-hundred-thousand-year existence, where we finally began to bottleneck and branch off into the various settlements that ultimately populated the globe. From there, our cultural differences began to take shape and form specific regional identities, complete with their own religions, weaponry, tools, art, etc. But almost every known human culture still contains each of those elements, however different from other cultures' equivalents they may be. These different cultures may have wildly different art, but they all

32

still have art—they understand the concept, and they find utility for it. Similarly, various weapons, tools, and religious traditions might differ from region to region, but each region nevertheless possesses some variation of the same concept of a tool, a weapon, or a god. These "similar differences," if we may call them that, show us that while diversity is real, said diversity shares fingerprints and qualities that make it universally human regardless of what particular form it takes.

Armed with this knowledge, modern cultural anthropologists can in many cases take what they learn about foreign cultures and find insights in that knowledge that can be applied to their own. As a result, ethnographies about specific regions can often reap universal truths about broader human behavior and tradition that can then tell us more about ourselves as a whole species. For instance, when ethnographer Victor Turner wrote his book *The Forest of Symbols*, he was compiling essays he had written regarding his fieldwork on the Ndembu people of Zambia in central Africa, but the book itself gave significant insight into how *all* human beings engage in the process of ritual and symbolism in their daily lives. Because of the data gathered and presented by Turner in that book and elsewhere, modern cultural anthropologists now have a clearer picture of how everyone in every culture might display reverence for symbols as representation for bigger, culturally linked concepts. In addition, this information has given us a better understanding of how cultures in general go through in-between periods of change bridging clearly defined states of being—a concept Turner dubbed **liminal states**. These concepts have broader application than it might first appear, and the field as a whole (as well as humanity's understanding of ourselves) becomes richer as a result.

Archaeology as a Scientific Grounding for Past Cultural Context

Keeping in the same tradition of empirical processes for all of the subfields of anthropology, archaeology as a subfield now utilizes scientifically backed methods for not only uncovering past artifacts of societies long past, but also determining what point in time said artifacts originated from. For this latter task, anthropologists use a technique known as **radiocarbon dating** to measure the amount of radioactive decay present in the bones and artifacts found at dig sites. This is done by measuring the amount of conversion that has taken place inside organic materials from an unstable (i.e. temporary) form of carbon known as C-14 back into nitrogen (its original form).

Let's take a step back and make sure this process is made as clear-yet-straightforward as possible. When nitrogen is bombarded with radiation from the Sun while hanging out in the Earth's atmosphere, it gets converted into C-14—colloquially referred to as radiocarbon. As the plants, animals, and other organic bodies that absorb carbon in life die and begin to decay, this process reverses and the C-14 found within the larger absorbed carbon eventually converts back into nitrogen. Radiocarbon dating is the process by which the length of time

The Scientific Turn

absorbed C-14 has taken to revert in this way is measured. Through comparing the amount of radiocarbon left in an absorbed total of carbon against the amount of unchanging carbon in that same total that doesn't decay (C-12), archaeologists and paleoanthropologists (evolutionary anthropologists who focus on digging up and analyzing human bones) can determine how old an artifact created through

ANTHROPOLOGY FOR BEGINNERS

organic materials is or how long ago someone was alive, respectively.

This process is very important to the overall field of anthropology because whenever a long-dead civilization or fossil is uncovered, the longer process of determining the cultural context of said discovery begins with determining, with empirical certainty, how far back in time the culture itself was existing and thriving. From there, cultural and linguistic anthropologists can come along and apply their respective expertise to further flesh out our understanding of the given culture being unearthed. But without that key ingredient of being able to determine the *when* of a given dead culture, the how and why cannot be properly contextualized.

How do we know it works? Well, following the scientific method, we can determine that carbon dating is a reliable and consistent tool for accurately determining the age of unearthed organic materials. Using other methods for determining the same thing, such as dendrochronology (measurement of tree rings), we can build a hypothesis (expected outcome) about what the radiocarbon reading of that same piece of material will bring. Since we want to determine the age of more things than just trees, the tree ring methodology has its limitations. But if carbon dating can accurately read the already-known age of a tree, for instance, then we can use tree ring dating to corroborate and prove correct the veracity of carbon dating. From there, carbon dating can be used to determine the ages of even more things that previous methods could not.

As it turns out, a process very similar to the hypothetical one just described is precisely what was used to prove carbon dating to be accurate and reliable— all the way back in 1949 by a pair of researchers named J.R. Arnold and W.F. Libby in their work,

But... I heard that carbon dating was inaccurate?!

The Scientific Turn

"Age Determinations by Radiocarbon Content: Checks with Samples of Known Age." Because the hypothesis that carbon dating would match other known methods of dating was proved correct, carbon dating was empirically shown to be reliable and scientifically accurate.

While some arguments against carbon dating as an accurate means of dating unearthed materials persist in layman circles, it is important to understand why such claims are being made and why they ultimately do *not* disprove carbon dating as scientifically sound.

For starters, it should be made clear that no scientific methodology is free of the human error and other natural limitations that come with every man-made endeavor. It is equally important, however, to remember that since nothing is free of such shortcomings, throwing out an entire practice, method, or field of study because of them would quickly deprive humanity of every beneficial scientific discovery, convenient invention, or artistic creation. In fact, the scientific method is designed with human error and natural anomaly in mind—this is why the emphasis on attempting to prove a claim *wrong* through repeated experiment and rigorous trial and error is so present in any scientific research undertaking. Carbon dating is no exception.

In other words, carbon dating works . . . except in the cases when it doesn't. But in those instances, the reason for an inaccurate date is not due to some innate shortcoming of the process of carbon dating itself; instead, the inaccuracies occur due to other external factors. For example, we aren't able to reliably carbon date artifacts beyond several thousand years due to the ultimately complete decay and dissipation of C-14 that occurs over time. Also, an external contamination of a given specimen could also cause the reading of contained radiocarbon to be thrown off. Nevertheless, when used within the right limitations and free of contaminants, carbon dating proves a very useful tool for dating unearthed elements from the organic past. Just like any other scientific methodology, it can only be applied in certain ways in order to get a correct result.

Aside from carbon dating, which is a type of **absolute dating** method, there are of course other dating methods used by archaeologists and paleoanthropologists to determine the ages of both organic materials whose radiocarbon content has long decayed away completely, as well as materials and artifacts that do not absorb carbon and therefore must be dated through other means. This kind of dating methodology is called **relative dating**, and it is done, simply put, through comparing an artifact or specimen of an unknown age up against an artifact or specimen of a known age. Despite the very interesting and beneficial nature of carbon dating, that methodology's aforementioned limitations actually necessitate that relative dating ends up being the most common means by which the majority of fossils' and artifacts' ages are determined.

If, for instance, one would find a fossilized specimen whose radiocarbon content had long withered away into nothing, and that fossil was located in or near a geological formation whose age has already been determined through other means, the scientists determining the age of the newly discovered fossil would then use the already known age of the nearby formation as their barometer. Now, if the artifact itself has additional information on it—let's say that it's not a fossil but is instead an old piece of pottery with esoteric markings on it—then that information can possibly be used to pinpoint an even more accurate determination of the artifact's age. But without the relative dating methods to significantly shrink the window of possible time in which the artifact itself could have existed, these subsequent narrowing down tasks cannot even begin.

Evolutionary Anthropology and Its Effect on Our Self-Understanding

There is arguably no greater framing for our collective understanding of humanity than the knowledge of our own evolution. Through the study of fossil records, genetics, and biology, evolutionary anthropologists can answer various questions about human anatomy that tie into our place in the history of the Earth as well as the where and when of our origins. The fact that we did evolve, and that we are merely part of a larger primate family tree, which itself has branched off from other trees of common ancestry further down the line, is a humbling one that keeps us aware of how precarious and extraordinary our journey to get here truly has been (and continues to be).

Understanding of how evolution works also plays a huge role in the medical world, and there are hyper-specialized evolutionary anthropologists called medical anthropologists who specialize in everything from human disease, medical trends within certain groups of humans based on the geographical clustering of their recent ancestry, and a phenomenon demonstrating culture's role in certain biological commonalities known as biocultural adaptation. There is also the forensic anthropologist, another specialized subset of evolutionary anthropologist, who examines remains and bones of the recently deceased for the purposes of giving scientific grounding to cause of death declarations in legal settings.

ANTHROPOLOGY FOR BEGINNERS

In addition to this knowledge, we also know through evolutionary anthropology that the concept of "race" within humans is actually completely non-existent at the genetic level, which means that it has only remained a credible stance in the cultural sphere; not the scientific one. But how do we actually know this? From the evolutionary end of this question, the answer is somewhat straightforward: there is simply no such thing as a "race" chromosome. The genetic information that determines things like outward physical characteristics is such a small portion of the entire genetic makeup of a person that it is entirely immaterial. This is called a phenotype—a trait that is visible but benign. Phenotypical differences are typically determined by external environmental factors. Just as with the earlier delineation of evolution within groups of the same species in chapter one using Darwin's Galapagos finches as the example, it is due to environmental location that certain physical characteristics end up winning out as being most common after hundreds of generations residing in the same climate and roughly the same spot on the planet. How our skin reacts to harsh sunlight exposure, for instance, or how naturally prone it is to contain melanin, which acts as protection from harmful UV rays, has been informed to how often a particular cluster of us humans have needed that particular trait to live long lives and give birth to similar-looking offspring. If we cluster in regions that have less exposure to those particular elements, over hundreds of generations the genetic trait that guarantees heavy melanin content in the skin dies out in favor of other, more useful traits in whatever region we happen to occupy.

This whole position of race being unscientific is of course further enforced by the knowledge (learned through fossil excavation and dating, as well as the charting of the human genome) that all modern humans trace back to African origins. In other words, phenotypical differences in outward appearance are only explainable through different climate exposure over time, and not through multiple origin points for all the different "races" that the early social Darwinists claimed were real and distinct from each other. Said multiple origin points simply do not exist, and scientific grounding of physical anthropology proves that.

Now that we have a better grasp of what the scientific turn within anthropology has brought us in terms of empirical knowledge about humanity, and how much this shift in approach genuinely benefitted the field at large, we can now dive into those findings themselves, across all four subfields, and trace our journey as a species—through space and time, and from the beginning all the way to the glorious, open-ended present.

BIOGRAPHY: Franz Boas

Born in Westphalia in 1858, Franz Boas was always interested in science as a means of understanding the human condition, though his academic studies veered him toward physics for his PhD in 1881. His dissertation on the color of water led him toward a better understanding of how perception of something empirically irrevocable can still be completely subjective. This was very applicable to the study of human culture and anatomy, where at the time the proposed reasons for surface-level differences were based on perception rather than empirical reality.

In 1883, Boas undertook fieldwork on Baffin Island in Canada in which its indigenous people, the Inuit, were determining certain perceived truths about their natural surroundings that were contrary to what Boas knew was objectively true about them through a physicist's lens. This was firmly in line with Boas's observations about perception of the color of water, only applied to culturally informed perception of

The Scientific Turn

natural phenomena at large. And just like the Inuit's cultural markers misinformed them about some of the things they observed, the same was surely true of academics in the West who were allowing their cultural biases to misinform them about the non-Western cultures they were observing and writing about.

Thus, cultural relativism was born, and with it, Boas's approach at a four-subfield reconfiguring of the field of anthropology at large. Boas published his studies on the Inuit, and with his new insights on cultural relativism became a new leader in the modern anthropological conversation. In 1896, Boas came to America and officially joined the faculty of Columbia University. It is there that anthropology's new life finally and fully took off. He stayed at Columbia until 1936, and along the way became a mentor to scads of budding anthropologists, forever changing the face of the field for the better as a scientifically sound discipline.

Unilinear evolutionism, the pseudoscientific "theory" peddled by the social Darwinists of the age that human cultures evolve in a linear fashion from primitive to advanced, was detested and rejected by Boas not just because of its lack of testability, but also because of its total lack of ubiquity. From culture to culture, no common threads of practices and knowledge of the inhabiting peoples could be delineated. This is a big part of what gave birth to the practice of ethnography—if one observes the culture and the people in question from a participant's perspective, the chances of misunderstanding the contexts or motivations therein reduce significantly. Boas knew that this would play a key role in defeating the social Darwinists at their own game: observation. Despite the title, Boas's book *The Mind of the Primitive Man* defines "primitive" in a very non-judgmental manner, stating that to be primitive in his eyes is to merely be part of a more uniform, less complex society than others. This in itself has no basis in biology, race, or language, and is rather informed by location, happenstance, and contextual need for survival utility. This, alongside the findings of Darwin himself in *The Descent of Man*, drew a line in the sand regarding the notion that evolution had anything to do at all with cultural sophistication.

Boas died on December 21, 1942, at an academic gathering comprised of himself and his peers. During lunch, he stood up, declared that he had devised "a new theory of race," and then collapsed into the arms of his fellow anthropologist Claude Levi-Strauss, forever robbing the world of his final development in the ongoing conversation of biology vs. cultural perception that had first ignited his career.

✦ 3 ✦

Early Humans

IN ORDER TO GET A BETTER GRASP OF WHERE WE CAME from, anthropologists have to take into account the information gathered about the much larger primate family tree we belong to. Primatology is therefore key in the anthropologist's arsenal of data, as well as genetics. The aforementioned fossil record and genetic code from the prior chapter makes it very clear: who are we? Broadly speaking, we ourselves are primates. And where we come from amounts to an incredibly rich line of ape-like ancestors that we share in common with modern apes that are alive today. That fact is sometimes difficult to unpack for someone who might not have ever considered this close relation before, so we can take a brief step back and observe the similarities of behavior among us and our primate cousins first before we dive into the genes we also share.

When was the last time you observed a chimpanzee? Was it at a zoo? Or was it on film, perhaps? In the former case, it is sometimes noticeable that chimps can behave similarly to people, but on film, this fact is exploited much more through use of anthropomorphizing said chimps with human clothing, trained gestures, using man-made objects properly, etc. This tends to delight us because it is uncanny just how human-like these apes appear. But why? We seem to be somewhat predisposed to find enjoyment in that sort of playful crossover between ape and man. If apes can mimic our behaviors so well with seemingly little adjustment to get there, then what is it exactly that divides us? Primatology examines this area of curiosity, and tends to

find evidence that in fact, we and our fellow primates are really not so dissimilar at all. We *are* primates just like chimpanzees and bonobos are also primates. We just happened to branch off and go a different direction than they did when we all began to evolve away from our shared common ancestor. But through the study of primate behavior, we can still see the evidence of our common traits of movement, motivation, and interaction.

Take for example a 2003 study out of the Yerkes National Primate Research Center at Emory University in which primatologists Frans de Waal and Sarah Brosnan were able to demonstrate that capuchins (an

Early Humans

adorable species of monkey made famous by the double agent character from the Steven Spielberg film *Raiders of the Lost Ark*) can understand (and reject) the concept of unequal pay. In the experiment cited in the study, two capuchins are trained to exchange marbles for grapes. The first capuchin does so without a hitch, and the second capuchin emulates what he sees the first monkey do and reaps the same reward. All is well. Then, when this cycle is repeated, a slight change happens: instead of a grape, the second capuchin is given a cucumber instead. Meanwhile, the first capuchin is still receiving grapes as his payment. The next time, it gets even worse for the second capuchin: the first one gets not one, but *two* grapes as his reward this time, while capuchin number two still gets one slice of cucumber for doing the same

ANTHROPOLOGY FOR BEGINNERS

work. When this injustice is carried out yet again in the next cycle, the capuchin that has been receiving cucumber slices rejects his payment, throwing the cucumber slice back at the scientist who handed it to him, and proceeds to throw a (very understandable) tantrum while his brother munches happily on his two grapes for doing the same level of work.

While this is adorable and relatable to watch, it is also very insightful regarding just how close we truly are to other primates in regards to how our lower-level, immediate responses and reactions to things we perceive as affronts to ourselves manifest.

None of this means we are exactly like our fellow primates, of course. And we humans are quite unique among the rest. But without contextualizing how we are unique yet still at home among a larger grouping of related primates, that uniqueness is less special. We can define what makes us human by delineating how we are significantly different from other apes while still recognizing our closely shared genetics as well.

So, what unique traits are these, exactly, among the entirety of primates? Well, for starters, we walk upright on two legs (bipedalism). We also craft and use tools. We also have language. And perhaps most significantly, we learned how to make fire. All four of these big defining characteristics also served as huge turning points along our evolutionary tract that veered us further and further away from our typical primate roots.

But are even these characteristics uniquely human? Similarly to anthropology, primatology has a handful of sub-specializations that focus on things like genetics, anatomy, cognition, behavior, etc., and some primatologists who specialize in behavior have argued that our closest relatives in the living primate family tree such as bonobos and chimps can in fact do some of these tasks just like we can. And indeed, there exists footage of bonobos building campfires and chimpanzees using human-made tools . . . when guided to do so by their scientist

Early Humans

observers. Which makes many scientists wonder if perhaps our ape cousins are merely very good mimics rather than our cognitive equals on these fronts. Nevertheless, it is still fascinating to see how genuinely similar we are to our closest primate relatives for them to even be able to mimic us as accurately as they do. We just happened to branch off and venture out in the way that we did once upon a time about a couple hundred thousand years ago—had things gone even slightly differently, we might not have ended up much more capable than bonobos at the whole crafting and fire-harnessing thing. And in case you were wondering, yes, it has also been shown that bonobos can successfully play video games once shown how.

In these instances, the way our culture has come to define us becomes more important at times than how perceived genetic limitations have doomed the other primates to so-called "sub-humanity." Circumstance, environment, and time. That is what has come to make us human. Much like Darwin's finches, we are the result of our surroundings and the random traits we just so happened to develop that proved useful for our survival. Ultimately, those initial traits gave us the physical and mental prowess to harness nature for our own benefit, and in that moment, we were no longer shaped solely by our surroundings and instead had means of maintaining our sustenance through "artificial" means such as tool crafting, clothing, and travel.

This splitting off occurred culturally and logistically, and the way our anatomy had evolved up to that point also played a role, but these outward changes that made all the difference for us have turned out to not be so genetically radical as perhaps we might have initially thought. With the sophistication of genetics as a scientific field as well as the mapping of the human genome, we now know for a fact that we humans and our closest ape relatives still share roughly 99.9% of the same DNA. The outward differences between these groups are broad, but the genetic reality is that we barely branched off at all in order to find ourselves able-bodied, talking, and designing skyscrapers. Technically, we ourselves are still apes, which means we still belong to one of the three main categories of primate: prosimians, monkeys (New World and Old World), and apes. But we apes, consisting of humans, bonobos, chimpanzees, gorillas, and orangutans, all took slightly different paths away from the earlier common ancestor we all originated from. This does *not* mean we used to be monkeys; it means we share the same origin point along with all of the great apes that are alive today. We evolved parallel to one another.

> **SAPIEN SIDELINE: THE INACCURATE MARCH OF PROGRESS DEPICTION**
>
> The very famous "March of Progress" illustration, whose proper title is The Road to Homo Sapiens, is actually quite infamous within anthropology. You see, it is scientifically inaccurate in that it depicts human evolution as a linear progression from ape to man and only further confuses everyday understanding of how human evolution actually occurs. Not only that, but it first appeared in a scientific publication (the Life Nature Library in 1965), which meant that it gave undo credence to the social Darwinist view that had already been long-debunked by anthropologists by then. Unsurprisingly, this image continues to prevail to this day as the most common depiction of human evolution that everyday people see. And we wonder why there is such confusion about how evolution works!

The Primate Family, Branch-By-Branch

But, when exactly did the entire primate branch of the evolutionary tree bifurcate away from our most recent common ancestor? What came before all of us primates was a sort of proto-primate creature that lived life in the trees—then, the first distinct primate grouping branched off about sixty million years ago, according to the fossil record. That line of primate would ultimately become the prosimians we know today (capuchins, tarsiers, lemurs, lorises, etc.). While they look barely anything like us humans, they are still primates just like us because they stuck around in our primate family tree long enough to remain primates by the time they branched off and became the distinct species that they are today. All but one of the distinct species of prosimians can be found in the Africa and India regions at large, while lemurs are only found specifically in the island country of Madagascar,

once again demonstrating how the population clustering in specific climates and locations over generations plays a role in which traits survive and thrive along the evolutionary journey.

Moving further along said journey, back on the main stem of the primate branch, we get another glimpse of our ancestors in the form of a fossil discovered by a farmer in the Hubei province of China—an early primate that showed distinct characteristics from the aforementioned prosimians. For one thing, more readily identifiable hands and feet were present, and the eyes were small like a monkey's; not large like the prosimians. Still yet, it was as small as tarsiers in its overall size, and serves as one of many transitional forms that has survived.

Early Humans

Roughly fifty-five million years old, this fossil (called Archicebus achilles) was only discovered in the year 2003. At the time of its discovery, it was the oldest salvaged primate skeleton, and it served to give significant insight into how early on the typical primate anatomy was evident. So, as we can see through the fossil record, after the earliest prosimians branched off, the rest of the primates kept going as well down a more uniform path for a few more million years—until the next branch-off occurred.

The next group to break off from the main primate branch was the New World monkeys (platyrrhini) around forty million years ago, and they can be found in Central and South America today. Their diet broadly speaking consists of fruit, vegetables, foliage, bugs, and other "light" foods of similar stock. Tamarins and marmosets are part of the New World monkeys, and through examining them, we can get a clue for how their regions of settlement over generations did not bring about the need for the same type of nuanced communication and intricate tool-making that our more recent direct ancestors would ultimately develop. Tamarins and marmosets don't have opposable thumbs, after all, nor can they change facial expressions. On the other hand, the larger types of New World monkeys such as the howler monkeys and capuchins have slightly more sophisticated movement necessitated by the specific regions *their* most recent direct ancestors primarily evolved from.

The New World monkeys' departure from the mainline primate branch of the evolutionary tree was soon followed by the Old World monkeys' earliest direct ancestors' departure about fifteen or so million years later. And that fifteen million years made all the difference in terms of how much closer in overall traits and characteristics the Old World monkeys are to us Homo sapiens. For instance, we and the Old World monkeys both have the same number and types of teeth—the first time that trait became locked in within primates. Why? Because for whatever reason, by the time and place that the Old World monkeys became a distinct species of primate, that extra molar that was still held onto by the New World monkeys was no longer needed for the kinds of food we and the earliest Old World monkeys were eating. Therefore, that particular trait no longer played a key role in survival, and it was ultimately left behind. Baboons are Old World monkeys—still not extremely close to us, but still much closer to us than, say, capuchins, or further down the line, lemurs. With each new branch off that occurs, we get closer and closer to the most recent grouping of primate: the apes.

Apes, while a general grouping of primates much like the others looked at thus far, are still very distinct amongst themselves. That's because the specific lines of apes still branched off slightly. Of the most immediately recognizable apes around today, orangutans are the furthest from us humans. Gorillas are slightly more closely related, but still branched off far back enough to where they are not our closest cousins. That title belongs to the bonobos and the chimpanzees, which are both roughly equally distant from us. This is because we were the ones to branch off after the gorilla about seven million years ago—or at least, our most direct ancestors were. As a result, we still share to this day roughly 99% of our genome with both the bonobos and the chimpanzees. By contrast, we share only about 80% of our genome with the prosimians, the earliest bifurcated line of primates.

All of this demonstrates, both through genetics and the surviving fossil record, that we humans are indeed primates—not just primates, but primates that come from one of the longest continual lines of evolution in the entire primate family tree. And yet, this complex relationship between us and our apes and primates at large is one not to be overly simplified by an appeal to linear progression. And through the scientific uncovering of our true line of evolution, we are able to put to rest the initial claims by the pre-scientific anthropologists that social Darwinism somehow holds water—it simply does not. And because we know that, we can more empirically inform not just our evolutionary anthropological research, but our social anthropology research as well. This is yet again an example of how all of the subfields of anthropology inform and bolster one another.

The Direct Ancestry of Modern Humans

Seven million years. That is how long it has been since our earliest direct ancestor branched off from our fellow primates. Think about that: seven million years. Can that even be easily imagined? And yet, in the grand scheme of things, we are a very new species compared to all life that has existed on this planet over its four-and-a-half-billion-year existence. Seven million years was still plenty of time, however, for us Homo sapiens to emerge and define as a distinct species of primate complete with our now-common features, customs, behaviors, and language. But somewhere along the way, there had to be a moment in which the first distinct human came to be . . . right?

Here, we have the conundrum of evolutionary speciation. Every fossil is a transitional fossil. Every living being is a transitional form.

ANTHROPOLOGY FOR BEGINNERS

The process is gradual, and evolution does not just happen within species; it causes different and new species to emerge, as well. And yet, because everything is gradual and always changing, there was never a "first human." We Homo sapiens simply came to be gradually, and we are still evolving today.

Paleoanthropologists, who specialize in early human fossils, do far more than just dig up bones. These hyper-specialized evolutionary anthropologists use their findings to determine the biology, anatomy, and culture of the earlier humans that are our ancestors. Through their work, we might not be able to pinpoint the so-called "first humans" (since, again, they do not exist), but we can certainly pinpoint when our ancestors started walking upright, and that is the next-best thing. This moment in our history serves as a threshold for when human-like behavior began to alter the lifestyles and aspirations of our earliest ancestors. And that moment, as has already been established, occurred roughly seven million years ago.

Early Humans

But again, how do we know this? Well, during a 2001 excavation in Chad in central Africa, paleoanthropologist Michel Brunet uncovered the fossil that plants this first major shift toward human-like characteristics in the seven-million-year mark. The fossil is known as Sahelanthropus tchadensis, or, "Sahelian human from Chad." At the time of its discovery, it was our oldest known bipedal ancestor. And how do we know that Sahelanthropus was bipedal (i.e. walked on two legs)? Why, from the way the spinal column attaches to the skull base, of course. This region of the skeleton is known as the foramen magnum, and it survived at the skull base of Sahelanthropus despite the rest of the skeleton no longer remaining. In the case of Sahelanthropus (and all bipedal primates), the spine connects to the skull from below, rather than from behind, which is what we see in the skeletons and fossil remains of primates who still walk(ed) on four legs. Some detractors to the claim that Sahelanthropus was a bipedal primate argue that its foramen magnum is still located too far back on the skull base for us to know for sure if the spine was indeed connected from underneath or not. However, as was pointed out earlier, there was no single primate that suddenly was "the first human." By that same token, there was no single primate that suddenly walked upright. Every being is itself a transitional form, and Sahelanthropus was no exception—the fact that its foramen magnum is still not smack dab in the middle of the skull base like a human's foramen magnum is therefore completely expected. A switch didn't get flipped to make primates walk upright; rather, happenstance and need for survival gradually dictated that walking upright was a useful tactic for some of them. In the case of Sahelanthropus, it is reasonable to surmise that walking upright had been a more recent development in its own direct ancestry, and therefore the foramen magnum would not yet have reached its most secure central location beneath the skull. Despite this, it is still evident that, early variation or not, the foramen magnum of Sahelanthropus is one that connected the spine to the skull from underneath rather than from behind.

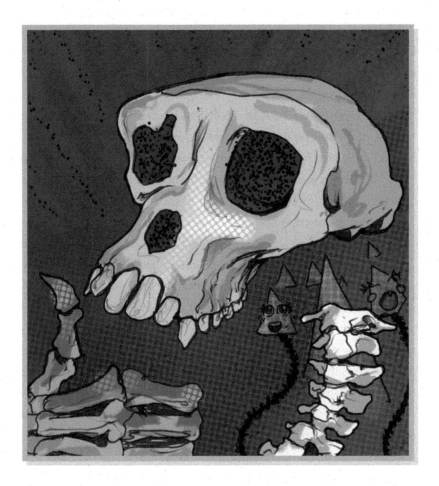

Whatever naysays might still bounce around in the ether regarding Sahelanthropus, a far less controversial fossil to be considered a direct ancestor to modern humans is the five-and-a-half-million-year-old Ardipithecus. Without a doubt bipedal, Ardipithecus was uncovered in Ethiopia in the early 1990s by anthropologists Berhane Asfaw and Timothy White. So fragile were the remains, however, that the team needed fifteen years to uncover and analyze it. CT scan technology was used in addition to the more typical methods, all in an attempt to not further damage what they had found during the analysis. The find amounted to a female skeleton that demonstrated a primate

Early Humans

both bipedal on land yet still capable of navigating in the trees. The full name of this find, Ardipithecus ramidus, roughly means "first grounded ape," or "root grounded ape." The name made sense at the time, since Sahelanthropus had yet to be discovered and therefore Ardipithecus was indeed the first bipedal walking ape in our direct line of ancestors yet dated. Again, the number and type of teeth found in this fossil was ever closer to the patterns found in our own. When an even older variation of Ardipithecus was found by the same anthropologists later on, *that* then became our oldest ancestor yet uncovered, earning it the sub-classification Ardipithecus kadabba. Science is constantly correcting, building upon, and refining its earlier findings, and in anthropology, this is blatantly evidenced in the ever-growing list of names for our early ancestors that often amount to the same meaning: this is the oldest version of ourselves we have yet found. But while the timeframe may continue to expand as we continue to find even older direct ancestors, the primary distinguishing factor we continue to adhere to is the characteristic of bipedalism—walking upright.

The label that has been given to these direct, upright-walking ancestors of ours broadly speaking is "hominin." And the hominin family tree has another distinguishing trait: it specifically took part in stone tool making at least as far back as two and a half million years ago, as evidenced by the currently unearthed archaeological and fossil record. Although, once more reminding ourselves of the ever-revising scientific foundations of modern anthropology, some further evidence has gone on to suggest that tool making likely occurred even earlier with Australopithecus, a four-million-year-old ancestor we will revisit in a moment in greater detail. Not only that, but chimpanzees are also capable of fashioning crude weaponry out of stone. All of this suggests that while hominids likely perfected a more *sophisticated* kind of tool making in the time (two and a half million years ago) and place (Ethiopia) suggested by the dug-up evidence in our direct ancestral line, the broader concept of creating tools for various proto-hunter-gatherer uses seems to have been present prior to our breaking off from chimps and bonobos.

Nevertheless, it is still notable that even if we take the more modest suggestion that true tool use among hominids did not become ubiquitous until roughly two and a half million years ago, that is even more astonishing in some ways. After all, two million years to graduate from spears and clubs to where we are now in the present in terms of our various engineering and architectural abilities is a tremendous amount of progress.

As promised, we will now dive into the very important discovery of the Australopithecine line of direct human ancestors. At first, Australopithecus was contested as even being a direct human ancestor despite its classifier, anatomy expert Raymond Dart, believing this to be the case. The variant he discovered, Australopithecus africanus ("southern ape from Africa"), was initially a one-off discovery in 1924, and thanks to the aforementioned scientific rejuvenation of anthropology by Boas outlined in the previous chapter, Dart's claim was (rightfully) met with much scrutiny and constant testing.

But after enough additional fossils in the Australopithecine line were uncovered after the initial discovery, anthropologists were able to compare and corroborate in order to definitively and empirically name this line of primate as indeed being a direct ancestor to us modern humans—or at least, many of the primates within the Australopithecine family were direct ancestors. In the case of Dart's africanus, it actually turned out that it was less directly related to us than other variations of Australopithecus that would be discovered later. Africanus, as it happens, branched off from the larger Australopithecine line before more directly related variants would continue along the path toward Homo sapiens. A much more directly related variant, Australopithecus afarensis, would be discovered later and give anthropologists enormous insight into the evolutionary echoes of our species. Most non-anthropologists know the afarensis variant by another name: Lucy.

BIOGRAPHY: Don Johansen

Donald Carl Johansen (b. 1943) was born in Chicago, Illinois, to Swedish parents on the 28th of June, 1943. Fascinated by anthropology since a young age, Johansen soon earned a bachelor's degree in 1966 from the University of Illinois at Urbana-Champaign. His master's and PhD would later be completed at the University of Chicago in 1970 and 1974, respectively.

A brilliant paleoanthropologist, Johansen quickly became a professor of anthropology at Case Western Reserve University. During this time, he set out on an excavation in Hadar, Ethiopia. His academic side was still in full gear, and he had to be pulled away last-minute from his writings in order to take part in the venture. What started out as a run-of-the-mill survey turned into one of the most significant discoveries in anthropology's history. In his peripheral vision, Johansen briefly spotted a bit of bone glimmering in the sunlight. It was fossilized.

Johansen could tell that the remains were hominin in appearance, but it wasn't until they were completely unearthed (a shocking amount of the skeleton was intact!) that they were identified as a type of Australopithecine. Not only that, but this type of Australopithecus was not the africanus variety of old—this was a direct ancestor to modern Homo sapiens, and it was over three million years old. Johansen and his crew celebrated the find in their tent later that night on November 24, 1974, and on the radio was playing the Beatles song "Lucy In The Sky With Diamonds." "To Lucy!" someone declared in an impromptu toast, and thus the skeleton had a name.

This variant of Australopithecus would be classified as Australopithecus afarensis (Latin for "Southern ape from afar"), and the discovery made Donald Johansen a scientist superstar. He would go on to found the Institute of Human Origins in Berkeley, California, in 1981, and is still revered as one of the leading paleoanthropologists alive today.

Over the course of this slow evolution along the direct line of Homo sapien ancestry, something else was in flux other than just our teeth, way of walking, and foramen magnum. The average brain size was also changing significantly, and while the seven-million-year-old Sahelanthropus might have walked upright like us, its brain capacity (as determined through skull size) was significantly smaller than that of modern Homo sapiens. In cubic centimeters (cc), Sahelanthropus had an average capacity of 400cc, while us modern humans have a capacity of 1,350cc. But again, evolution is not a ladder of objectively linear progress from "primitive" to "sophisticated," and so it is worth pointing out that our brain capacity actually used to be a bit larger than what it is today about thirty thousand or so years in the past. But as our needs for survival became more and more specific and refined, so did our physical forms—including our brains. We developed the areas of the brain that were most necessary for survival and special preservation, ultimately discarding the areas of the brain that matters less to achieving that end. Think of it like a sculptor filing down his statue in order to better refine its most appealing qualities and get rid of the excess marble that serves no purpose to the end goal of the sculpture standing the test of time against the elements.

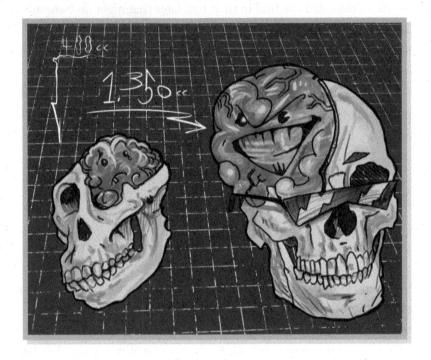

Before we discovered Lucy, but after Australopithecines at large had already been established as legitimate, the aforementioned tool makers from two and a half million years ago were discovered by anthropologist couple Mary and Louis Leakey. Their discovery helped cement the growing notion at the time (this was the early 1960s) that all humans originated from the African continent, as there were no other fossils of the same time period that could be directly connected to humans in the same way anywhere else on the globe.

The fossil in particular that the Leakeys found was initially thought to be the origin point of sophisticated tools for hominids. Therefore, the name Homo habilis, which literally means "handy man," was only fitting. But as has been the observed trend so far with this whole naming business, later discoveries would go on to revise these initial claims, and our "handy man" ancestor would go on to be revealed as more of

Early Humans

a refiner of existing technology rather than the innovator of it himself. Nevertheless, the discovery of Homo habilis still brought anthropologists even closer to piecing together the puzzle of our direct ancestry along the bifurcating evolutionary journey.

As the decades went on and we found Lucy, Sahelanthropus, etc., the notion that Homo sapiens' direct ancestors all originated from Africa became more and more empirically provable, as all of these fossils were found on the African continent and nowhere else. In addition, these fossils when lined up according to their dated origins told a story spanning seven million years leading into our present form, meaning that for a very, very long time, the direct line of human ancestry remained in Africa before early Homo sapiens finally did begin to migrate and go elsewhere.

But before we finally turn to that chapter of our early human story, we still have yet one more stage of direct ancestry to go over: Homo erectus. Being the most recent of all the aforementioned ancestors thus far (dating back to around 1.9 million years ago), it was also the first to be discovered—all the way back in 1891, nearly a decade before Franz Boas would ultimately refine anthropology at large into an exclusively empirical discipline. As such, it was not a professionally trained paleoanthropologist who made the first discovery, but rather a Dutch surgeon named Eugene Dubois. Without the later empirical data that would go on to prove Dubois's discovery to be an early human, Dubois simply assumed it was a strange bipedal ape of some sort. He gave it the initial title of Pithecanthropus erectus—"ape that stands erect."

Once even more fossils of this newly discovered variant were discovered, and as the empirically trained paleoanthropologists applied more and more scrutiny to their analyses of said findings, it became clear that this was yet another direct ancestor to Homo sapiens—our most recent yet discovered! The renamed Homo erectus earned its own classification distinct from Homo habilis because it contained qualities unique enough to warrant its own place along the evolutionary tract of direct human ancestry. For one thing, the brain of Homo erectus

ANTHROPOLOGY FOR BEGINNERS

had the capacity of 1,000cc—significantly more than Homo habilis, and certainly more than the even earlier ancestors. Also, the tools being used by Homo erectus were even more sophisticated and varied than anything that had come before. Homo erectus was a "thinker," and this evidence proved that. Finally, some variations of Homo erectus would go on to be found outside of Africa—the very first direct human ancestor to have breached that continent's boarders. And as we next turn to the migration path of the earliest Homo sapiens, we will see that this was a huge new development in hominin behavior. In other words, Homo erectus (and its Asian and European variants) directly paved the way for Homo sapiens both in migration patterns as well as physical characteristics and intellectual application. It is the most

Early Humans

similar to our previous direct ancestors, and given the fact that it is also the most recent of our direct ancestors, that fact makes complete sense.

Now that we have finally caught up to our present form, Homo sapiens, we still need to break things down once more in order to better understand the evolution that we ourselves went through from our earliest emergence onto the scene up to now. To do this, anthropologists tend to separate sapien history into two eras: the archaic and the contemporary. The archaic fossils we have thus far uncovered are all located in Africa. This means once again that, as of this writing, the only evidence anthropologists can empirically determine regarding our origins is the evidence to suggest that *all* human beings originated from Africa before migrating ourselves in the same fashion as Homo erectus. What this means is that regional adaptation within contemporary sapiens is the leading explanation for variation in skin tone and other phenotypical (surface-level) differences in appearance across regions. The fossils of our archaic sapien ancestors, combined with the genetic data of our contemporary form, also prove that we modern humans are all one single race.

And what is that race? The only living hominins left: Homo sapiens. We are survivors. We choose to bend nature to our own needs as a means of survival rather than letting nature itself determine what traits lead to thriving or extinction. This is a trend built upon those who came before us with their stone tools and initial decision to walk upright and traverse the ground below the trees. We owe a great deal to these ancestors of ours for taking the first steps toward bucking our nature and using our intellect to outthink our present circumstances. But once our present form arrived on the scene, what came next?

The Migrations of Early Homo Sapiens

Like Homo erectus before us, we humans would ultimately migrate out of our documented origin point of Africa and into Asia and the Middle-Eastern regions. From there, we kept going and found the

Americas. But this process was slow and arduous, and there was (contrary to popular belief) more than just one single migration of sapiens out of Africa. Erectus was very far-reaching when it came to its kind's migrations, but it never made it quite as far as we did before its extinction. The fossil record has yet to uncover any evidence to the contrary, as no surviving Homo erectus fossils have been found in the Americas or northern Europe. How Homo sapiens outlived Homo erectus is still hypothesized even today, but relatively recent genetic evidence has shown that most non-African modern humans actually contain an average of 3% Neanderthal DNA. What that means is that once Homo sapiens left Africa, they interbred with their Neanderthal cousins in order to strengthen overall numbers and build alliances.

Early Humans

But wait a second—what are Neanderthals? Well, what *were* Neanderthals would be a more accurate phrasing of the same question. You see, even though non-African humans technically have remnants of Neanderthal DNA, we must remember what else was made a point of earlier—we are all still one species and race. The leftover Neanderthal DNA present in a certain geographical population of humans does not mean that those humans are somehow less human than their African counterparts. Ultimately, speciation did not occur and Homo sapiens still ended up winning the genetic tug-of-war. Neanderthals themselves, and this is very important, were a subspecies of human still located in the broader genus Homo. Meaning that they originated from the same line of direct ancestors as we humans did. They were *not* a different species altogether, or else we would not have been able to breed with them. Neanderthals were by all accounts excellent hunters, toolmakers much like us, and even had very large brains—although it is hypothesized based on cranium remains that Neanderthal brains were more hind brain than front brain, which might have significantly limited their higher reasoning skills compared to Homo sapiens. In any case, the evidence now shows that they interbred with us in an attempt to survive, yet ended up going extinct anyway as Homo sapiens grew more numerous and won out in genetic resilience along the line of the subsequent offspring. This, combined with the already touched upon intellectual ability of early Homo sapiens to buck their nature and bend the natural resources to their will as a means of surviving otherwise unlivable climates and temperatures, contributed to our survival beyond the rest of our genus Homo peers. The more scientific label for this explanation of how Homo sapiens outlived our fellow early humans during the migrations is known as the Partial Replacement (or Assimilation) Model. It was one of a few competing hypotheses for how this happened, but again, with the arrival of the genetic evidence of interbreeding, it is now more resilient than ever as the most empirically sound explanation.

As was laid out earlier, there were multiple migrations out of Africa

ANTHROPOLOGY FOR BEGINNERS

by early humans, Homo sapiens included. As for *when* Homo sapiens first left Africa in this said migration era of our species? Well, a finding of nearly fifty human teeth in Beijing, China, in 2015 proved that early Homo sapiens had left Africa at least as far back as one hundred thousand years ago! Think of it—one hundred thousand years to spread

from Africa to the rest of the world. Plenty of time for various population clusters and bottlenecks to form along the way and form roots in specific regions. Plenty of time for those population bottlenecks to establish their own unique cultures and art; for their outward physical appearances to shift as they interacted with different climates for generations on end; for region-specific written and spoken languages to emerge. By this point, it should be more obvious than ever as to why

Early Humans

Franz Boas's decision to ground anthropology in scientific empiricism was so necessary. With the genetic data and fossil records we have gone on to uncover in the century since that shift, we have been able to demonstrate the real reasons for why humans look, act, and speak so differently based on what region of the globe they inhabit while also being able to determine why we are all still one species, one race, and one surviving branch of a much larger genus Homo—the most resilient of the remaining apes. General skin color, eye shape, hair texture, etc. are simply minute adaptations to the elements for specific region populations that dropped anchor along the way during this great period of migration some one hundred thousand years ago. And we know this not just because of the fossil record, but also because of genetics.

Have you ever heard of Mitochondrial Eve? What about Y-Chromosomal Adam? If not, you really should. Both of these individuals lived a very long time ago back in Africa prior to these aforementioned migrations occurred. They are also directly related to every single living human today. Y-chromosome DNA, as most entry-level biology classes will tell you, is found in males and it is passed down the male genetic line from father to son, generation to generation. The earliest we can trace this back to through genome mapping of modern humans is around the same time these migrations began to take place—roughly a hundred thousand years ago. Nicknamed "Y-Chromosomal Adam," this most recent common ancestor (on the patrilineal side) for living Homo sapiens can prove on a genetic level the same thing the fossil record suggests: that all living human beings trace back to that single place and time. Similarly, "Mitochondrial Eve," the most recent common ancestor for all living humans on the matrilineal side of things, also corroborates the fossil record's story. Why the mother's side exclusively? Because when a human egg is fertilized, the sperm's mitochondrial DNA (the DNA inside a cell that serves as the "engine" for keeping it alive) does not enter the egg along with the rest of the sperm's DNA. Because of that, the only mitochondrial DNA that ever gets passed down to offspring is that of the mother. While

ANTHROPOLOGY FOR BEGINNERS

Y-Chromosomal Adam might date as far back as one hundred thousand years, Mitochondrial Eve traces back twice as far: two hundred thousand years. Yet more evidence that all surviving humans trace back genetically to Africa exclusively.

Once again, multiple scientific approaches and fields have come together, compared, adjusted, and either confirmed or denied the hypothesis in question as a means of further solidifying the empirical certainty of anthropology's claims. That is real science doing real work to better clarify our understanding of ourselves and our origins. A far cry from the early days of explorers writing their initial impressions of foreign people in their journals. So much for the hypothesis of the so-called "primitive" man vs. the "modern" man. The scientific reality is that we are all evolving together, parallel to one another, with only geographical location and climate to account for our surface-level differences.

Speaking of climate, you might have heard something before about this little thing called the ice age. Much like the migrations out of Africa, it turns out that there was actually more than one ice age. But the most recent one is what is often being referred to by the aforementioned colloquial term. What that amounts to is the fact that the most recent mass glacial overtake of large continents was about thirty thousand years ago, and it affected early humans' migration patterns and pacing in a big way. Remember those population bottlenecks we touched upon earlier? Well, one of those bottlenecks occurred in Siberia, which for a very long time was the final stop for migrating Homo sapiens since the glacial expansion at the time hindered any further traversal. Then, about ten thousand years later, the ice melted, making way for Homo sapiens to travel farther than they had before—into the Americas. The fossil evidence we currently have shows that at least as far back as twelve thousand years ago, Homo sapiens were exploiting that new route and settling down in the Americas. Northern Yukon's Bluefish Caves, located just west of the Americas, houses archaeological evidence of big-game hunters and butchers living on the edge of these glacial barriers around twenty-five thousand years ago. Beyond these

Early Humans

barriers around the same time we have no evidence of any sort to suggest that these same hunters and butchers resided in the Americas. Around ten thousand years later, however, that completely changes and we see both archaeological and fossil evidence of migration past that initial barricaded area and into the Americas. Places like Fort Rock Cave in Oregon and Murray Springs in Arizona, for instance, house such findings. And this makes perfect sense, as the timeline of human migration into the Americas matches the timeline of the ice glaciers leading from Siberia to the Americas melting down and clearing a new path.

More than just the dating of these findings, however, tell anthropologists the story of a direct migration. Something else that supports this version of events is the fact that the archaeological evidence across all of the Americas, Central and South America included, shows that for thousands of years, all of the early humans residing in these regions shared the same exact toolkit for hunting and foraging. For instance, there is a very specifically designed spearhead in this region known as the Clovis point (named after the place in New Mexico where the first examples of them were uncovered in 1929). Fluted in its design and made of stone, the Clovis point is found around the same time in North America, Central America, and northern South America, making it very simple to trace a direct migration from Siberia into the Americas at large, then south, all around fourteen to twelve thousand years ago. The Clovis point itself is something of a technical marvel given its age, and marks yet another instance of early human ingenuity. The fluted design

Early Humans

means that a functional notch is present at its base, making it attachable and detachable along spears and arrows of differing sizes. Such a multifunctional piece of tech was obviously useful to these early hunters, and the fact that the Clovis point is found across all three continents of the Americas demonstrates that it served the survival and propagation of its wielders very well. Who first found the Clovis point? An archaeologist? Believe it or not, it was stumbled upon by a teenager—Ridgley Whiteman. Ridgley now has a dedicated entry in encyclopedias for this chance discovery!

ANTHROPOLOGY FOR BEGINNERS

On the genetics side of things, it has also been confirmed that these "Clovis humans" share a direct lineage with modern Native Americans. However, in light of remaining open to further evidence continuing to refine our scientific understanding, some anthropologists dedicate their studies to seeking out evidence of possible "pre-Clovis humans" in these same regions, since we do know that multiple migrations, and not just one, spread Homo sapiens across the globe.

Something else that is even more fascinating about all of this is how we as an entire species can remain so uniform yet so simultaneously differentiated, culturally speaking. This apparent contradiction becomes much easier to understand, however, once we look at all of the evidence laid out in this chapter and realize that we all share a single origin point prior to our bifurcation across the rest of the globe outside of Africa. The Clovis humans of the earliest Americas' societies all had their special variation of the spearhead, yet many other cultures elsewhere on Earth have spears. The same thing goes with different variations of bows and arrows, blades, clubs, clothing, and other general survival resources. You might recall at the beginning of this book how we examined the fact that various societies all have a broadly homogeneous concept of art, culture, and religion, yet differ quite greatly from one another in the specifics from place to place. The same principle is active in both the cultural aspect as well as the practical. Many different places on Earth were weaving fireside tales of dragons (or their close variants) at the same time. Just like they were fashioning their own versions of arrows and spears at the same time. The reason why these broader parallels exist while the dissimilar details prevail is because of these aforementioned migrations. From a common point of origin, the beginnings of human culture were sparked. From there, as the migrations occurred and different populations clustered at different points and began to form unique identities over thousands of years, those initial sparks were kindled into different yet similar fires that burned into the histories and identities of

Early Humans

thousands of nations. But as these differences became formed over time, our common ancestry, as well as our common human cultural outlook, now has the empirical backing to make sense of how and why we can be so different yet remain one race—the surviving members of genus Homo. Humans. And as we turn to our modern understanding of ourselves, these facts surrounding our early commonality need always remain in our minds.

◆ 4 ◆
Modern Insights

TODAY, WE HUMANS FIND PLENTY OF REASONS TO DIVIDE ourselves. Whether it be politics, nationality, religion, taste in art and entertainment, our economic status, or this ill-conceived concept of "race," the ways in which we are different tend to take the spotlight more often than the ways in which we are alike. But as we have seen in chapter three, the scientific evidence is clear: we are

all one race with one common place of geographical origin. Time and migration came to give us our surface-level diversity as we interacted with different climates, temperatures, and sun exposure, but at the molecular level, we are all together.

This does not mean, however, that anthropologists can therefore dismiss the importance of race as a concept. Remember, anthropology is as concerned with the cultural side of humanity as it is with the biological, and the unfortunate truth is that "race" is still seen as a valid means of categorizing people in most societies today. While it has no scientific grounding, this approach of assuming innate uniqueness within different groups of people based on phenotypical differences (i.e. differences in outward appearances exclusively) has gone on to have massive cultural effects that can be measured concretely.

Many anthropologists have tried to unpack this truth within the subdisciplines over the years—among them, archaeologist Charles Orser in his 2004 book *Race and Practice in Archaeological Interpretation*, in which he determines that anthropologists in his subfield have historically confused the abstract label of "race" with more tangible concepts like ethnicity (place of origin) and social class (socioeconomic status within a given culture). Other anthropologists have tackled the race question from both biological and cultural angles, such as Alan H. Goodman, Yolanda T. Moses, and Joseph L. Jones in the 2012 work *Race: Are We So Different?*

What we find through these multi-directional investigations of race throughout time and space is that while race in and of itself is a culturally invented concept with no biological grounding, society still operates as if it is real. As such, mass assumptions are still made to this day that inform behaviors and treatment from person to person based on things like skin color, ethnicity, and national origin. Think about it: if the false idea that a person with a certain nationality is fundamentally different than you has been ingrained in your mind by everyone around you from birth, would you not be more prone to treat said person differently and hold that person to different expectations?

ANTHROPOLOGY FOR BEGINNERS

And as a result, would this person of different nationality not be more likely to experience life differently once multiple people treat him the same way that you do?

This is where cultural anthropology becomes an invaluable tool in understanding how people of different skin colors, nationalities, religions, etc. can be the same as their peers genetically, yet still experience a completely different social and economic existence simultaneously. This is because culture matters. A growing trend in the age of enlightenment was to reduce everything we experienced in the natural world to a matter of scientific empiricism (explaining the "how" of things)— even when that approach was not capable of fully explaining the "why" behind certain cultural phenomena. Today, this mindset lives on in some circles that put raw data collection above everything else, keeping it free of cultural or social context. This mindset is often referred to in scholarly circles as "scientism." What anthropology is uniquely equipped to do, as opposed to other scientific fields, is avoid this pitfall by both gathering said raw data but then proceeding to contextualize that data in the social experience. The issue of race is a perfect example of how this has been done with relevant results. Anthropology can determine on the hard science side of things that race is not biologically sound, yet at the same time, cultural anthropologists can continue to measure and study the very real social effects of that false concept being perpetuated in everyday life. Both realities are relevant, and together, equally weighted in importance, they can affect positive change in the public perception of what race is and whether or not it actually matters. Separating the cultural from the biological understanding of race and only focusing on one or the other in isolation keeps this very necessary conversation (and subsequent revelations) from happening. Modern anthropology being both a social *and* natural science means that such conversations stand to happen much more often when anthropologists study concepts that cross over between the two worlds.

Modern Insights

Anthropological Insight on Family and Kinship

What else can social anthropology give us insight on? Well, many things. But we can continue to look at the findings that have an effect on the big everyday social concepts we tend to take for granted—race is only one of them. What is another? Well, what about family? Is that also an exclusively biological reality? For many decades, even after anthropology's scientific turn, the assumption was yes. But as ethnographers, the empirically minded participant observers who study foreign cultures, gathered more and more data about the cultures they were studying, they came to uncover a greater truth: that family has just as much input from culture as it does biology. In fact, "kinship" is something that is oftentimes chosen based on social norms or customs in some cultures that go back much further in time than modern

ANTHROPOLOGY FOR BEGINNERS

Western cultures. Of course, direct bloodlines have also been used to determine kinship and family hierarchy for just as long elsewhere in the world, but this has not uniformly been the case. And that is the point. Once again, we must take off the ethnocentric glasses and embrace cultural relativism when it comes to our preconceptions of what constitutes family relation. In the West, the non-biological concept of family has been harder to warm up to, while elsewhere in the world it has oftentimes already been the norm.

However, in 1997, American anthropologist Kath Weston published her book *Families We Choose*, which put a new focus on how non-biological kinship had manifested in the West—right under the noses of the more traditional naysayers. In Weston's research, it was shown that many households and sub-communities of non-traditional genders and sexual orientations had already embraced the idea that family should be seen as a nurturing circle of people who care for and love one another through thick and thin—regardless of whether or not they are blood related. This makes a lot of sense of the cultural front, even in the West, since at this time marriage equality in America was still decades away from national legalization and many LGBT people were still living lives affected by blatant discrimination. Perhaps even more tragically, these same demographics of people were also losing ground in their private lives through being disowned by their biological family members. What other choice did some of these individuals have other than to embrace a non-biological concept of family and belonging? And through doing so, they found a truth that other cultures had already been living—one just as real, relevant, and functional as the concept of bloodlines also constituting what makes a family. Either way, "family" and "kinship" find their active definitions through cultural language: love, belonging, caretaking, teaching, nurturing, and so forth. Whether one starts with a biological or cultural basis for what "family" is, these common concepts of what a family looks like in practice are consistent. Once again, this is not something that the natural sciences alone can give insight on, and yet, it is just

Modern Insights

as true when experienced in daily life by human beings who for one reason or another happen to fall outside the predetermined boxes we think they should belong in based on our previous science-exclusive postulations about what makes people related to each other.

This new understanding of kinship, though now backed up through both Western and non-Western documentation, as previously mentioned, fell on deaf ears even within the reformed anthropology field for a while, largely because the conventions of everyday life had still not been challenged as often as they are now. Even one of the most

ANTHROPOLOGY FOR BEGINNERS

(rightfully) revered anthropologists of all time, Claude Levi-Strauss (who we will learn a bit more about later), assumed that a society's sense of culture and cohesiveness was contingent on the nuclear family unit remaining intact. But remember, anthropology is now informed by scientific empiricism, where testing and correcting existing claims in the field is ultimately encouraged and celebrated. At long last, the conventional assumption about what true kinship can look like was challenged enough to warrant further data collection, and we now have a much broader understanding of what "family" truly is and can be as a result of that research.

Anthropological Insights on Sex and Gender

Much like race and family, something else that was culturally assumed for centuries as being already fully understood and unshakeable, gender, would come to be challenged by scientists in various fields, including biology, neuroscience, and psychology, but also by anthropologists, who again have the unique position of seeing both the cultural and scientific implications of studying such a dense topic.

To fully understand gender as a whole concept with all of its complexities fully laid out for complete dissection, one must consult a volume specifically dedicated to the subject. However, the shorthand explanation of why gender was even called into question in the first place from the strictly anthropological side is quite simple: we have uncovered evidence that proves other cultures outside of the European traditions were recognizing the existence of more than two genders for centuries. Certain Native American societies recognized five genders, for instance, while Hawaiians have long had an officially recognized third gender, "mahu," which covers a wide range of people possessing non-binary characteristics, biology, and behavior. The more literal translation of this word amounts to something along the lines of "intermediate state between male and female," and in pre-colonial

84

times, the mahu were healers and seen as wise and powerful. In certain East Asian regions, trans females are seen as goddesses. "Hijra" in India and Pakistan is the classification for people of obscure or transitional physical sex, such as intersex and trans people, and they have long been legally recognized as such. Elsewhere, in Polynesia, the "fa'afafine" are non-binary people who are assigned male at birth yet demonstrate a spectrum of gender behavior that rangers from the ultra-masculine to the incredibly feminine. They not only exist and receive official everyday recognition, but they are an integral part of Polynesian tradition.

But, how can this be? Is a person's gender not determined by their biological sex from birth? Believe it or not, this assumption is a relatively recent and heavily Western phenomenon. Historians have identified the apparent origins of this perspective in a culture referred to as "scientia sexualis," the tethering of medical science's understanding of genitalia

ANTHROPOLOGY FOR BEGINNERS

to one's gender identity. And socially, that expectation has become second-nature and largely unquestioned in the West as a result. However, many other regions with very little to no Western cultural influence do not share that same cultural understanding of sex and gender, as has been demonstrated from the examples above. In these cultures, gender is largely **performative** and external. Behavior and self-perception have more to do with a person's gender in these regions than what biological sex organs said person happened to be born with. The assumption that male and female genders are the only genders that a

Modern Insights

person can possibly perform or perceive themselves as is just that—an assumption. And anthropologists have played a part in proving that to be the case by evidencing the numerous examples of this assumption being rejected or contradicted elsewhere.

But even moving into the realm of human biology makes this question of sex and gender less clear cut than one might expect if one possesses only a high school level understanding of the subject. That is because beneath the surface-level distillation of X-chromosomes and Y-chromosomes dictating a person's genitalia, there is the far more complex reality that genitalia itself occurs on something of a spectrum, and it can at times manifest as either obscure or simultaneously male and female on a single person. In these cases, Western *culture*, not medicine, has determined that every person can only be one sex or the other. As a result, babies that are born with both genitalia are usually manipulated by their doctors through plastic surgery on the genitalia and injection of hormones from a very early age to then conform to the Western cultural concept of binary gender being directly linked to an equally binary sense of sex. This has gone on to psychologically harm the non-binary children in question, as their own self-perception of what gender they are might not end up matching what gender their doctors chose for them. Nevertheless, the Western assumption even today is that gender and sex are linked, and that both categories are binary and locked. Despite the cultural and biological evidence to the contrary, this assumption is one of the most fiercely clung-to traditions in the modern West.

Fortunately, the fields of psychology and neuroscience are starting to provide anthropologists with even more scientific evidence in favor of gender being a multifaceted phenomenon that exists separately from biological sex. We now have brain scans, for instance, that show people who identify as transgender in the West possess wholly unique physical brain structures from cisgender (non-trans) people's brains. But the thought to even look at the brain for confirmation in the first place stemmed from the fact that gender as a binary concept was being initially challenged on the cultural front, and that anthropologists had centuries of cultural evidence pointing to the reality that non-binary gender norms existed.

Anthropological Insights on Money

Economists have long argued over what the so-called natural state of markets are in society. Is capitalism an organic phenomenon that occurs when top-down forces choose not to intervene? Or is it fairer to simply craft an economy that distributes money and wealth in a way that is equitable to all people based on their socioeconomic status?

Modern Insights

These debates all make an assumption, however, that markets are innately money-dependent. After all, isn't it the incentive of getting paid that motivates people to trade goods and do favors? Anthropologists challenged this assumption, and questioned whether or not there existed other origins and motivations for the concept of mutual exchange. Namely, Marcel Mauss, the nephew of the even more famous anthropologist Emile Durkheim, took on his contemporaries regarding the notion of monetary fuel being the only mover of markets in society.

So, Mauss decided to do his research elsewhere—outside of the West (which, as we have established by now, gives great insight for anthropologists interested in a culturally relative perspective). His time studying what were considered "archaic" societies from around the world, with a special emphasis on cultures of the Pacific Northwest, resulted in his 1925 work *The Gift*, which would later be translated to English in 1954 (Mauss, like his uncle Emile Durkheim, was French). The findings were extraordinary: the concept of mutual exchange exists entirely outside of the idea of currency, which proved the suspicion that something more innately human about exchange of goods and services exists even in regions of the globe that do not have a concept of what most of Mauss's colleagues in the West considered the most important ingredients of a market system: money.

What Mauss discovered was that the desire to give, receive, and most importantly, reciprocate, seems to exist innately across all humanity, while the justification to do so originates in various different mindsets that are informed by the culture and customs of the region in question. Some cultures see a gift as being a piece of the

Modern Insights

giver's soul, and therefore the obligation to give back to the original giver is a matter of keeping said person's soul complete. Other cultures under Mauss's microscope were shown to see exchange of services and good deeds as being a form of social capital—the potlatch, for instance, is a ceremony that is usually held by a local chief or other social luminary in which various material goods are given to others or done away with as a gesture of opulence and wealth. It then becomes the desire of participants to return the favor and hold a potlach of their own—if only to match the same sense of social importance and wealth as the original host.

The modern insights here should be fairly easy to spot—in terms of the mutual exchange observation made by Mauss, it stands to reason that money is not the inception of market exchange in the West as was originally thought, but is instead the Western world's own form of retrofitted rationale for why we want to exchange goods among ourselves. In this way, we aren't much different from the cultures Mauss observed; we are merely a variant of this same custom that takes the currency used in the exchanges incredibly seriously as its own self-contained power. As for the Western variant of the potlatch, how often do we in our own place and time pine over an other's wealth and way of life? How often do we feel as if we have not succeeded in life and social status until we too possess the big house with the big yard and entertain our neighbors with expensive parties?

But this idea of social status being reflective of one's character and importance also has another major origin point in the West—the Puritan work ethic. This was something fully delineated by yet another European researcher—this time, a German. His name was Max Weber, and in his book *The Protestant Ethic and the Spirit of Capitalism*, he pointed out the connections between the idea of wealth and accumulation of capital as being seen as proof of favor in the eyes of God. This was something the various Protestant sects of northern Europe (and, subsequently, settlers in the early colonized Americas) pushed their fellows to aim for—if one built an economically resilient enterprise

ANTHROPOLOGY FOR BEGINNERS

in the tangible, secular world, they argued, it would serve as proof that God rewarded their hard work and gave them blessings while here on Earth. In other words, according to Weber, the Protestants played an unwitting role in the perpetuation, spread, and normalization of modern capitalism. Weber's book went on to be considered one of the founding texts of economic anthropology, and it was listed in 1998 as the fourth most important sociological work of the twentieth century (it was published in 1905).

Between the work of both Mauss and Weber, and their colleagues who would continue to develop their initial findings, anthropology and sociology were opening the concept of monetary markets as organic and constant up for significant challenge and debate. We had evidence of other non-Western cultures treating markets entirely differently, but we also had through Weber's work an explanation as to why the Western mindset of markets as being innately connected to capital accumulation became as ubiquitous as it was in the first place.

That isn't to say, of course, that no cultures besides those in Western societies ever embraced the concept of currency. On the contrary, many others did, as well. But they each had their own culturally engrained reasons for doing so. And of course, anthropologists post-Boas being interested in empirically backing up their claims, we have unearthed archaeological records that can help us better understand the how and why of these other cultural perspectives. For one thing, this evidence heavily suggests that we humans understood the concept of credit well before money itself—yet another counterintuitive notion in the eyes of monetarily minded Western scholars.

But what else can we gather about the earliest use of exchange in human culture? We know thanks to Mauss that various reasons are given from culture to culture; great, but what causes it in the first place? Since it precedes money, we have to dig deeper—into our genes. Biological anthropologists have been able to prove, for instance, that humans, like many other animals, possess something in our DNA that gives us what is called a rudimentary number sense. This sense isn't so

92

Modern Insights

much an innate ability to count as it is an ability to instinctually sense the concept of more or less of something. There are various instances in nature of animals displaying this ability by routinely gathering the same exact amount of food needed for themselves and their offspring each time feeding occurs. In humans this sense is also present, and it

manifests as an ability to comprehend the concept of numbers even before numbers themselves are introduced. Infants, for instance, understand when something has been added to or taken away from a larger group of the same item. The term "number sense" as seen in humans was coined by the late great mathematician Tobias Dantzing in his 1930 book *Number: The Language of Science* as an observation. But it was the work of anthropologists that, in the words of Tobias, corroborated his notion of its existence, demonstrating how indigenous tribes of people in Australia who had no formal knowledge of numbers beyond rudimentary finger counting still possessed the ability to tell quantity.

These findings, combined with what have been uncovered about early commerce by Mauss, show that money itself is not the genesis of exchange value or cultural reverence for reciprocation. Capital gains do not drive markets like Mauss's contemporaries once thought; instead, it is innate abilities within human beings to detect the concept of loss and gain combined with unique cultural perceptions that first brought broad stroke free market ideas like value, personal betterment through exchange, social connections and status, and so forth, to humanity at large.

Even now in the most contemporary of scholarship, anthropologists (most notably David Graeber) continue to study the origins behind fiscal and commerce concepts that are taken for granted today as having always existed, uncovering very interesting pieces of evidence that suggest that much of today's capitalist economy is essentially a reworking of feudalism in which class divides are perpetuated for socially informed reasons rather than biological ones. The human proclivity to exchange and reciprocate goods and services, it seems, is not the same thing as the social imposition to tether this innate tendency to economic hierarchy. And understanding this difference is only something as uniquely equipped as the multi-disciplined anthropology can clearly do.

Anthropological Insights on Social Order and Individualism

Anyone who even dips a toe briefly into the anthropology pool will likely soon enough encounter the following terms: functionalism, structuralism, and of course, structural-functionalism. The meanings behind each of these terms tend to be somewhat convoluted across the anthropological literature, mainly because as these concepts were

Modern Insights

developing, their meanings often changed or refined within relatively short periods of time.

So, let's try to break them down. Firstly, it is important to note that all three of them are concerned with unpacking the often complex relationship between individuals, groups, and the societies they inhabit and interact within. The difference between the functionalist perspective, the structuralist perspective, and the structural-functionalist perspective really stems from what angle said relationships are examined from.

To understand functionalism as it is most commonly defined within the field, we first need to understand who promulgated it. Bronislaw Malinowski was essentially the European equivalent of Franz Boas. While Boas was the person to stress the importance of ethnography at the outset, it was Malinowski who helped shape the specifics of the process and constraints of the participant observation practice itself. Functionalism in the Malinowski tradition is therefore very concerned with individual and the constraints that social institutions impose upon them. Conversely, structuralism was traditionally understood in

ANTHROPOLOGY FOR BEGINNERS

anthropology as being far more concerned with the grander concepts of whole groups of people, social institutions, etc., and how they all fit together to comprise the whole of human society. To a structuralist, how a person experiences culture in isolation is immaterial compared to the overall purpose that individual serves when taken as part of a group. There are even some anthropologists today who still operate on the concept that individuals don't truly exist, as they are all informed by the groups they are part of and the culture they help create through these interactions.

Structural-functionalism, an invention of a man named Alfred Radcliffe-Brown, is a kind of synthesis of these two seemingly incongruent ideas into a more holistic approach that marries both individualist observations and social interaction among groups. Another well-known anthropologist, Emile Durkheim (Marcel Mauss's uncle), greatly influenced the work of Radcliffe-Brown, as did the anarchist author Peter Kropotkin, both of whom argued that interaction between all of society's elements, individuals and groups included, all served specific purposes in keeping human society running like a well-oiled machine, and that social institutions were just as important as the individuals who comprised them. Durkheim explained this as being akin to the organs of a human body always needing to be kept healthy and functioning properly in order for the whole person to be healthy as well. Radcliffe-Brown took this idea and ran with it, arguing that "society" and "culture" were distinct things that at the time were more indistinguishable in the contemporary literature. Boas's concepts of culture and society were to Radcliffe-Brown muddy and got in the way of truly explaining the how and why of human society's clockwork-like order. Culture, argued Radcliffe-Brown, came from a person's need to function within and make sense of society, while society itself was comprised of the people, places, and institutions that made everyday life a reliable routine.

However, despite Radcliffe-Brown's apparent need to make this distinction when examining Boas, it should be noted that Boas himself and his followers were in fact working on this same problem, with their concept of enculturation (or what today is called socialization) essentially arriving at the same conclusion as Radcliffe-Brown on this front.

Today, structural-functionalism continues to inform current anthropological study whenever the purpose of certain cultural practices is the subject of inquiry. And it was the combined work of various anthropologists on both sides of the "debate," as well as the unifying work of the likes of Claude Levi-Strauss and Radcliffe-Brown, that we can ultimately thank for the richness of this approach.

BIOGRAPHY: Bronislaw Malinowski

Bronislaw Malinowski (1884–1942) was born in Krakow, Poland, while it was still considered a province under the rule of the Austro-Hungarian Kingdom of Galicia and Lodomeria. His parents would have been considered more of an elite class than most, his father being a professor and his mother hailing from a land-owning family, but despite this, Malinowski never lived a horribly privileged life. As a child he was always ill, which got in the way of any real hope of a high-class social life. In place of this, he turned to academics, which he excelled at right from the start. His first university pursuit was in the study of applied mathematics and philosophy, and that led him to a PhD in mathematics of physical sciences in 1908.

However, during another sick spell at the very university he obtained his doctorate from, Malinowski stumbled upon the book *The Golden Bough* by anthropologist James Frazer. This book examined magic and religion through an anthropological lens, and from that point on, Malinowski was hooked. He decided to shift his academic focus and become an anthropologist himself.

Malinowski would go on to contribute to the development of ethnography into a scientifically sound research practice, delineating the details and processes of participant observation. In 1910, he took on more formal education, this time focusing on the social aspect of exchange, at the London School of Economics. As a result of his dedication to making ethnography an empirical, reliable process, he became one of the most acclaimed studiers of social systems, having brought anthropology "off the verandah," according to his contempo-

raries. Marcel Mauss's work on exchange in *The Gift* also built upon foundations laid by Malinowski with his study of the Kula ring and its cultural significance involving reciprocity. Aside from Franz Boas, Malinowski is arguably the most important figure in modern anthropology's inception.

Malinowski's brilliance and importance to his field went on to earn him a faculty position at Yale University in New Haven, Connecticut. He would remain there until his death. Sadly, that death was very untimely—just before he was expected to go do fieldwork in Mexico, Malinowski died suddenly of a heart attack at age fifty-eight.

BIOGRAPHY: Alfred Radcliffe-Brown

Alfred Reginald Radcliffe-Brown (1881–1955) was born in Birmingham, England, with only the last name Brown; "Radcliffe" would be tacked on later to give reverence to his mother's maiden name. The son of a clerk, Radcliffe-Brown was no stranger to the struggle of the every man and how education and academia could play a role in improving everyday life. In college, he earned the nickname "Anarchy Brown" due to his affection for the writings of anarchist thinker Peter Kropotkin.

However, Radcliffe-Brown would go on to explain that he read the likes of Kropotkin, Bakunin, Proudhan, and other classical anarchists because they too were men of empiricism, and that the sentiment of Kropotkin that any successful attempt to improve society should be preceded by a scientific understanding of it truly spoke to him and influenced his own empirical approach at anthropology.

Radcliffe-Brown is a bit of a contradiction when it comes to his work on kinship. While he was among the first scholars to argue against bloodlines being the only means of socially recognized family relations (and he stood in firm opposition to Claude Levi-Strauss's theory of alliances that argued families only form for mutual personal gain and social status), he still didn't quite reach beyond the confines of the nuclear family when it came to his concept of the ideal structure of households. Children needing two parents, the parents being male and female, etc., were still seen as the norm even in anthropological circles at the time, and Radcliffe-Brown did not do much to challenge this.

Nevertheless, the legacy left behind is clear, and the field of anthropology is all the richer thanks to the work of Alfred Radcliffe-Brown, yet another early adopter of scientific empiricism in anthropological study.

Anthropological Insight on Language

Linguistics as its own field did not always find itself informed by anthropology, nor was the contrary always true. But when the linguist Ferdinand de Saussure presented his lectures that would later become a transcribed book, *Course in General Linguistics*, in the early 1900s, the

Modern Insights

connections between language and culture were irreversibly made in scholarship.

Structuralist themselves in presentation, Saussure's ideas on how language itself informs cultural experience (and vice-versa) were ground-breaking at the time. In short: Saussure postulated that language as an isolated thing all to itself is an illusory notion, and that culture itself is deeply intertwined with it. Saussure put a focus on synchronic language (as it exists at a specific point in time) rather than diachronic language (language as a constantly changing thing through time), whereas most of his contemporaries were doing just the opposite. By freeze-framing language as it exists in specific times and places, Saussure was able to demonstrate how cultural influence comes to define meanings of words as psychological perceptions rather than mere labels of material realities.

To explain, Saussure visualized the concept in the form of what he called the "sign." The sign itself is two-fold: it contains both the signifier (or "sound image"), and the thing being signified (or the "concept"). Within this construct, the signifier is the literal word (for example, the word "cow"), while the signified thing is the concept associated with the word (for example, a visual representation of a cow). The reason why this distinction is important is because many of Saussure's contemporaries felt that words were simply labels that we put on things that are themselves tangible and unshakeable. There was no cultural underpinning to these words; they were simply one-to-one linguistic equivalents of real things and concepts that already exist out in the world. But if that were truly the case, argued Saussure, then there should be no essential difference between how many words we use to describe a given thing when we look across cultures. Yet, this is not the case at all.

For instance, in the English language, there is one word to describe a cow. The word is, of course, "cow." But what if that animal is slaughtered and turned into food? Is the same word used? No. Instead, we use the word "beef." There is a similar difference between live and slaughtered pigs and chickens: "pig" vs. "pork," "chicken" vs. "poultry,"

ANTHROPOLOGY FOR BEGINNERS

etc. One might say this is because a live animal and a cooked portion of that animal's meat are two distinct things, and therefore it only makes sense for distinct terms to be used for each. However, it isn't that simple. "Poultry," for instance, covers more than just chicken in its cooked state, and yet doesn't account for all bird meat. "Duck," for instance, is used for both live ducks and cooked duck meat. A similar trend is seen with the word "fish." And not only is this inconsistency found within just one language; these trends don't even match up across different languages. Some languages use the same word for both live and cooked pig, for instance, but not fish.

And these examples stretch far beyond just animals and their foodie forms. There are some concepts in certain cultures that don't even have single words to describe them in one language, yet do have single word descriptors in others. For instance, there is a word in Japanese, *gekkokujo*, that embodies the concept of a socially lowly person

Modern Insights

managing to raise himself up above cultural expectations and become a much higher socially regarded person. In English, there is not an equivalent word, even though the concept itself can still be described using multiple words. These examples are just a few among many that demonstrate how incorrect Saussure's fellows were at the time about the one-to-one labelling nature of language. Instead, as was exemplified through his diagraming of the "sign" concept, Saussure was able to show that language and culture heavily inform one another and that what represents a given thing is not, in and of itself, that thing—it is merely a symbolic representation or placeholder for it, and as a

ANTHROPOLOGY FOR BEGINNERS

result cannot be divorced from the cultural elements that inform it at a given time or place.

But this was not the only major leap forward that was to happen for linguistics in the twentieth century. Indeed, in the 1950s, a young American linguist named Noam Chomsky submitted to the linguistics department at the University of Pennsylvania, his undergraduate alma mater, his theory for what would eventually come to be known as universal grammar. The theory is very straightforward: like number sense, the ability for human beings to intuitively understand and work within language seems innate and untaught. Specifically, Chomsky demonstrated that humans, even toddlers without prior knowledge of language "rules" taught in school, already understand the grammatical structure of language. In fact, if one were to put two toddlers together without prior knowledge of any existing language, they would proceed to communicate through impromptu verbal means and co-develop a sort of made-up language to serve the function of communication. And yet, even without prior experience with existing languages, those toddlers' made-up language would still possess grammatical structure. There would still be subjects, verbs, direct and indirect objects, nouns, a clear foundation regarding in what order these elements should come in a sentence, and so forth. This phenomenon is more broadly known as the poverty of stimulus (POS), and it serves as very compelling evidence for the existence of universal grammar. For putting forth this argument and demonstrating it as well as he did, Chomsky earned his PhD in linguistics right there on the spot. His submission was taken as a doctoral dissertation.

Even today, Chomsky has continued to build upon and refine his theory of universal grammar, and is now more convinced than ever that there is a biological basis for why human beings already seem to have this language-building ability hard-wired into our brains.

Modern Insights

BIOGRAPHY: Ferdinand de Saussure

Ferdinand de Saussure (1857-1913) was born in Geneva to very brilliant parents. His father was a taxonomist and mineralogist, and Ferdinand was apt to follow in his father's academic footsteps. He studied at the University of Geneva at a very early age after already learning Classical Greek and Latin, then went on to graduate studies at the University of Leipzig. By age twenty-one, Saussure had already published his first book.

ANTHROPOLOGY FOR BEGINNERS

Eventually, after researching, traveling, and teaching himself even more languages, Saussure would return to Leipzig in 1880 to defend his doctoral dissertation and finally earn his PhD. He then went on to teach at various institutions for over two decades.

Saussure presented his lectures on the topic of language's relationship to social perception and interactions. These lectures were later transcribed and published posthumously as his *Course in General Linguistics* in 1916. It singlehandedly transformed linguistics forever, marking one of the first times such clear ties between language and culture were made that did not depend on the study of language's change over time. Instead, Saussure's focus was on how language in a given time and place is always informing words themselves, what they actually mean, and how they are used in relation to the places, things, and concepts they represent.

Today, Saussure remains one of the most quoted linguists in history, and almost all of the modern work in the field uses Saussure's concepts as its foundation. He died in Switzerland at the age of fifty-five, before his most Earth-shattering work even saw publication.

BIOGRAPHY: Noam Chomsky

Avram Noam Chomsky (1928–present) is an American linguist, cognitive scientist, and political theorist who is most widely recognized for two major things: his theory of universal grammar, which argues that human beings have an innate, untaught ability to recognize and abide by ubiquitous grammatical language structure, as well as his contributions to political theory and social commentary.

Chomsky's universal grammar bombshell was dropped in the 1950s when he was still a young student at the University of Pennsylvania, and it changed the field of linguistics forever. Dr. Chomsky has continued to refine this theory over the years, and many aspects of it

Modern Insights

have been shown to be applicable to computer language programming and cognitive science (even more evidence that it is largely a correct explanation of human language ability, as theories become more and more successful the longer they go without being disproven by subsequent research). Most recently, Dr. Chomsky co-wrote a book called *Why Only Us* with computer scientist Robert C. Berwick in which a simplified mechanism for human language construction, called "merge," is attributed to a biological mutation that is unique in Homo sapiens and likely occurred very suddenly—around 40,000 years ago, around the same time that art and culture seem to also spring suddenly

ANTHROPOLOGY FOR BEGINNERS

forward in sophistication in the archaeological record. Once again, the combined data across various subfields of anthropology plays a part in piecing together this complex puzzle of the how and why behind modern humanity.

But Dr. Chomsky's contributions to the thinking world do not stop there. He is also revered as one of the most brilliant social theorists alive today, and has written just as many acclaimed works in that field as he has in linguistics. One of his most famous books in the social sphere, *Manufacturing Consent*, demonstrates how many social facts in present times are imposed upon people through the mass media rather than organically from within, while still managing to masquerade as the latter.

While his theory of universal grammar is still not completely accepted by everyone in his field, and while his social commentary has its political foes, it can safely be said that through his work on both fronts, linguistic and social, Dr. Chomsky is one of the most important contributors to anthropological data of the past century.

Anthropological Insight on Social Norms

Emile Durkheim coined the term "social fact" to describe a cultural norm that goes on to dictate social behavior and control at large. In this sense, things such as gender roles, monetary systems, religious practices, art conventions, and many other taken for granted norms (both covered in this chapter and beyond) can all be considered social facts. These are concepts that end up transcending the individual experience and go on to dictate the daily order of things in a given society. Social facts, therefore, are arguably the key ingredient that serves as the connecting tissue between culture and society.

It wasn't just Durkheim who wrote about these things, of course; Claude Levi-Strauss, the famous French anthropologist, delved into

Modern Insights

understanding this aforementioned connective tissue for much of his career. His most famous book, *Tristes Tropiques*, was published in 1955 and served as an examination of, among many things, the effect of development on the environment, and then subsequently of the environment of cultural perception and norms. Levi-Strauss would ironically go on to reject the breakthrough work on kinship that called into question the social norms of the nuclear family (itself a concept developed by Radcliffe-Brown in an equally shortsighted stroke of ethnocentrist assumption), but was nevertheless brilliant and integral to social anthropology's continued development and sophistication into the twentieth century.

> **BIOGRAPHY: Emile Durkheim**

David Emile Durkheim (1858-1917) was a French sociologist who played a big role at the turn of the century in grounding social science in general in a more empirical approach of study. Though he is no longer as big of a direct influence on modern anthropologists as he was in the early twentieth century, his legacy still looms large and many of his initial ideas were expanded upon and revised by anthropologists later on.

Modern Insights

Durkheim coined many terms and phrases related to social study that have now become ubiquitous in common language. One such term, "collective consciousness," derives from his belief that social phenomena should be taken holistically when studied rather than broken down to the level of the individual person. This of course would differ from some of his contemporaries and ultimately be reworked by his structural-functionalist successors, but nevertheless, Durkheim's influence on the study of various social topics including hierarchy, stratification (i.e. a cultural justification for things like class divides and caste systems), morality, and deviance can still be felt to this day.

While born Jewish, Durkheim would go on to lead a fully secular existence and even study religion as a social phenomenon rather than a practice related to something actually divine. His work on religion would eventually become less relevant in the wake of the Mary Douglas ilk of social anthropologist, but still invaluable as a solid foundation upon which such seminal works could be built.

World War I had challenged his resolve to remain nuanced and non-nationalistic throughout his life, which made him less than popular among many peers. His loss of a social life, accompanied by the deaths of many of his students-turned-soldiers as well as his own son, proved too large of a collective toll on his emotional and mental well-being. Durkheim died from complications of a stroke in November of 1917 at age fifty-nine.

BIOGRAPHY: Claude Levi-Strauss

Claude Levi-Strauss (1908-2009) was a French **ethnologist** who arguably became the most high-profile anthropologist of the twentieth century, and who is credited alongside Franz Boas as being something of a father to the modern form of the discipline. His work *Tristes Tropiques* earned him much of the aforementioned fame for serving as a

window into what Levi-Strauss called "a human society reduced to its most basic expression," again giving insight into the ways of the West through examining other, seemingly "primitive" cultures.

But this work was very different from what most would consider a full-blown ethnography by today's standards, even though Levi-Strauss was indeed among the people he was writing about. The work itself is still presented as an amalgamation of various journeys, contextualized much like ethnographies, yet compiled together to create a broader sweep of cultural overview than what a traditional ethnography would be. This stems from the fact that, again, Levi-Strauss's specialty was ethology rather than ethnography.

While an ethnography is an in-depth, long-term research project driven by participant observation within a specific group of people, ethnology is the practice of taking the research already compiled from existing ethnographies of various groups of people and comparing and contrasting between them. Arguably, this step in the process toward unpacking and appreciating the connections between all humans is invaluable and renders ethnography far more useful than it would be on its own. As such, *Tristes Tropiques* serves as a kind of mid-point between ethnography and ethnology, as in this case, Levi-Strauss was essentially doing ethnology using his own data.

In addition to his academic achievements, Levi-Strauss's push against ethnocentrism put him in a socially conscious ilk that would earn him praise from outside of his immediate anthropological circle for the rest of his life. He received countless honors, including honorary doctorates from the likes of Harvard, Columbia, and Oxford, and was on the whole a major intellectual force in the fight for a fairer world. He died in October 2009 at the age of 100, at the time the oldest member ever of the Académie Française.

Anthropological Insights on Religion and Folklore

While many scholars over the past century and beyond have all contributed in various ways to the study of religious tradition and its accompanying stories and histories, there are two in particular who have examined these elements of humanity in the world of anthropology that are worth highlighting: Zora Neale Hurston and Mary Douglas.

Hurston in particular was interested in the connections between southern American and Haitian folklore and those regions' surrounding histories. She did ethnographic fieldwork and wrote extensively on these topics while a student at Barnard College at Columbia University.

ANTHROPOLOGY FOR BEGINNERS

Her mentor was Franz Boas. She published an incredible work, *Mules and Men*, in 1935, that housed collections of folklore and accompanying commentaries connecting them to their cultures and histories.

Hurston's real fame, however, came from her work as a fiction writer in the Harlem Renaissance literary tradition. There, she found a place in history alongside the likes of Langston Hughes as a master storyteller and artist. But her work as an anthropologist, while lesser-known to the masses, played a huge role in developing our understanding of how folklore is informed by culture and history, and vice-versa.

Mary Douglas was likewise an integral figure in anthropology's understanding of folklore and religion, but in her case, the connections made were between these beliefs and certain rituals, customs, and mindsets regarding normalcy or degeneracy in everyday life. Her most famous work, *Purity and Danger* (1966), was a dissection of what is seen as cultural purity vs. pollution as it ties into religious influence on the common zeitgeist of modern societies. It is considered a key work in social anthropology even today.

BIOGRAPHY: Zora Neale Hurston

Zora Neale Hurston (1891–1960) was born in Alabama, the sixth of eight children. Her father was a preacher and sharecropper, and her mother was a teacher. Her grandparents had been born into slavery. This history of her people was very close to home for Hurston, and from an early age she became intrigued in getting a better understanding of how that history affected the day-to-day culture of black Americans.

Throughout her younger years, Hurston struggled to reach her more scholarly goals while dealing with caring for her family and dealing with her mother's death as well as the general pushback that young women of color would have received during this time. At a much older age than she even let on (she lied about her birth year to keep attending

high school), Zora Neale Hurston graduated high school and finally set off on her academic ambitions.

In 1920, Hurston earned an associate's degree from the historically black college Howard University. There, she had studied various languages, done public speaking, joined the honors society, and founded *The Hilltop*, which is still to this day the official student newspaper of Howard University. Her accomplishments landed her a scholarship to Barnard College at Columbia University, where she became a mentee of Franz Boas and earned her BA in Anthropology in 1928. She was thirty-seven years old.

ANTHROPOLOGY FOR BEGINNERS

Hurston's subsequent fieldwork on the American South shed new light on what she identified as "paramour rights," in which white slave owners during that time of history were assuming the right to use their female black slaves as means of sexual partnership and mothering of children against their will. While this sinister fact of history is oft-referenced today in many works related to slavery in America, Hurston's work on the matter was one of the first serious scholarly acknowledgements and explorations of its impact and implications.

While her work was invaluable and her brilliance undeniable, her gender and skin color meant that she would never find the respect she deserved in life as a serious anthropologist. She never completed a PhD, nor was she brought into the contemporary anthropological conversation. Despite all of her work and ambition, it was still a world that was not yet ready to accept her. She found fame in other avenues as a fiction writer and an important figure in the Harlem Renaissance movement, but her anthropological work would not be taken seriously until after her death in 1960, itself a result of her not finding the success and financial stability she always wished for. Health complications that she could not afford to manage led to a stroke and subsequent heart failure. But her legacy now looms larger than ever in both the literary and anthropological worlds.

BIOGRAPHY: Mary Douglas

Margaret Mary Tew (1921–2007), more commonly known as Mary Douglas, was born in Italy to very devout Roman Catholic parents. Brought up in the faith all through her schooling, Douglas became interested in religiosity and its effect on human culture. While working in the British Colonial Office later in life, she came into contact with many social anthropologists and decided that their work was the sort of thing that could give her the insight she was after.

Douglas went to Oxford to study anthropology professionally. In 1949, she had registered to earn her doctorate in the subject. In the early 1950s, she completed said degree and went on to teach at the University College, London. She held that position for over two decades while simultaneously conducting various fieldwork and writing major books on said work that gave great insight into various topics such as commerce, warfare, and of course, religiosity's effect on social concepts of purity.

Douglas published *Purity and Danger: An Analysis of Concepts of Pollution and Taboo* in 1966 to much praise and respect. In it, she focused on concepts such as "dirt" in a philosophical sense that comes from religious concepts of pollution of purity and how it manifests in everyday social practices. Things such as religious diet, for instance, came about because of lack of information at the time making it difficult to neatly categorize certain animals in ways that felt manageable at the time, according to Douglas. As pattern-seeking mammals, us having a problem with this lack of clarity makes sense. In the end, clarifications between things like sacred, clean, and unclean are put forth in the book, arguing that unique origins exist for each category, and that these origins can differ based on time, place, and conditions.

Douglas died of cancer in London in 2007. She was eighty-six years old. Her influence remains in anthropology's approach to understanding religious customs and social perceptions, and without her work, social anthropologists at large would be significantly behind in the overall journey toward understanding how social norms grow, change, and interact with culture and history.

Modern Insights

Anthropology, when pivoted toward a sociocultural investigation through its social anthropology subfield, has proven time and again to better explain and further our understanding of the human condition as it exists in the space of cultural norms, social interaction, and individual-group dynamics. But as has also been demonstrated thus far, it is never just one single subfield of anthropology that does all the work. The insight on the social front that anthropology brings us is not just through social anthropology, but rather through a very intricate interweaving of social, linguistic, and biological anthropology so that we may better understand a given social phenomenon through all possible angles and not fall prey to any blind spots that an otherwise one-dimensional focus of inquiry might lead us into. As we continue to better understand the richness of the field, it becomes increasingly important to also come to grips with the reality that it is its unique blend of social and hard sciences that make anthropology the invaluable field that it is and can continue to be moving forward—especially as we march deeper into the fog of sociopolitical discourse and hot button debates of the current century.

✦ 5 ✦

Four Subfields, A Unique Advantage

AS HAS BEEN DEMONSTRATED ELSEWHERE IN THIS BOOK, anthropology's utility as a field of inquiry is best understood as a kind of mediator between the social and the academic; the artful and the scientific. The fact that social sciences and hard sciences are often seen as diametrically opposed areas of academic expertise in their mindsets and methodologies is a woeful tragedy. And yet, that has become increasingly the norm in the everyday public perception.

Just look at any politically charged debate or conversation today. Often, the slogan "facts don't care about your feelings" gets thrown about like a mantra that is somehow meant to instantly help the person using the term "win" the debate at hand. The accompanying assumption of this phrase is that the person using it is basing his or her positions off of empirical data, whereas the opponent must be building the counterclaim on a much shakier foundation. Often, the person with the supposed facts on his or her side is seen as citing "science," while the opposing debater is perceived as being "merely" a social scientist. But what is really going on here? Is there really such a major divide that cannot be reconciled between, say, a sociologist and a neuroscientist? Or are both fields equally relevant in what they have to say?

Anthropology happens to be a field that has one foot planted in each arena—both social science and natural science. As such, it is uniquely advantaged to see connections between the two worlds that

Four Subfields, A Unique Advantage

other fields that operate exclusively in one or the other cannot intuitively grasp.

For instance, the aforementioned issue of "race" and how anthropologists know it is a socially constructed concept. Anthropologists only know that right away because they have both biological and social anthropological data to reference when studying the same topic. It is approached from both ends, and together, both subfields work to provide the puzzle pieces. Race is not something that can be defined biologically, but at the same time, the label that we consider to be "race" is applied according to phenotypical differences between certain groups of humans. We categorize ourselves and each other because that is something we have always culturally and socially done. It behooves

ANTHROPOLOGY FOR BEGINNERS

us to recognize that reality and not discard simply because we now know that race doesn't exist. Both facts are equally true: race does not exist, and yet society behaves as if it does. If we appealed exclusively to the hard science fact of the nonexistence of race, we might be in danger of completely dismissing out of hand the equally true reality that a perceived difference between races has led to incredibly inhumane treatment of certain groups of people throughout human history and even today. Since anthropology does give equal weight to both its social and natural scientific wings, that pitfall is avoided and the issue of race is studied holistically.

This unfortunately is not always the case in other fields that have an exclusive focus on either the hard or soft science subjects. An example of how the race conversation in particular can be damaging without taking both hard and soft science findings into account is when some psychologists decided to draw lines of correlation across perceived racial differences when examining the average results to the IQ test. The assumption from the outset in this case was that race was in fact a tangible thing that biology can determine. This of course is not true, and so, categorizing anything based on "race" is completely useless. Yet, because those psychologists didn't communicate with the biological anthropologists at the outset about the race question, this error was never caught, and the IQ test results were averaged according to "race" anyway.

The result? A very controversial book called *The Bell Curve*, in which the claim was made that "black" Americans are less intelligent than "white" Americans because the average black IQ test score was lower than the average white IQ test score. This distinction means nothing, since race isn't a genetic reality. And yet, because the social and natural science worlds remain so devoid of communication, this fundamental misunderstanding of what race even is on the scientific front remains to this day. And there have been plenty of sinister actors since *The Bell Curve*'s publication who cite it as "science" and "facts." And this claim continues to go unchallenged because the worlds of social and

Four Subfields, A Unique Advantage

hard sciences rarely talk—imagine how many points of confusion and misinformation could be cleared up and avoided respectively if they simply did?

In anthropology, that conversation already happens, and both the social and hard science sides of the field hold each other accountable to their respective findings. It makes for a very socially conscious yet empirically sound body of work—something that is useful both to scholars and to everyday people. Because the data itself is not simply presented on its own in a vacuum; it is gathered, then measured against how it manifests in cultural spaces to determine what social implications can be drawn from it.

What results from this approach is a field that examines things like political movements from an objective perspective yet still doesn't lose sight of why political stances matter. To be clear: political conversations are important because of the social effects that result from them, but even more important is whether or not the foundations of these conversations are empirically sound in the first place. That is where anthropological study of political movements and mindsets is concerned: where the empirical origins and motivations for said positions reside.

For instance, the work of anthropologist James Ferguson in his 1990 book *The Anti-Politics Machine* was not interested in picking political sides of a given debate; it was, however, concerned with determining the cause of what Ferguson identified as an anti-political populist

mindset that breeds distrust of authorities within humans. And Ferguson did this through fieldwork in Lesotho where he looked at the bureaucracies in play in that region and traced the distrust of said bureaucracies within the everyday people to specific instances of failed development projects. The powers that be promised growth, stability, better quality of life, extended commerce, etc., and then failed to deliver on that promise time and again. Through these experiences, the people of the region grew to distrust the rhetoric of their leaders in business and politics. This provides insight into not just the political zeitgeist of Lesotho, but of anywhere in the world where this sort of distrust is bred through similar means.

What we come away with when books like Ferguson's challenge our understanding of political mindsets is the knowledge that, regardless of how extreme or incorrect a given political movement may be in its rhetoric, reasoning, or actions, there is usually an origin point for said movement that can be empathized with across political lines as a shared human experience. Understanding that first and foremost gives a clearer window into how to better clarify for research purposes the motives and behaviors of people who align with certain identity politics or populist movements. And none of this requires that anthropologist doing this work participate in the politics himself. But understanding the properly contextualized underpinnings of observed political phenomena is something that anthropologists are already more equipped to do compared to a political pundit or journalist who might already be operating on a world of assumptions and politically informed biases that will be taken for granted as fact. It is this more empathetic view of humanity that also gives clarity to the phenomenon of the **diasporic** communities of dispersed migrants from their relative places of birth who come together to form new merged cultures that themselves earn their own contexts and social practices unique to them.

Without the four-subfield approach of grounding all social research in scientific empiricism, anthropology would be a poorer discipline on the whole. And the same goes for the contrary: if biological

ANTHROPOLOGY FOR BEGINNERS

anthropologists or archaeologists kept their findings in the lab or on the dig site and failed to converse with their social anthropologist brethren, their findings would lack significant context and have much less utility in the everyday world. Together, these subfields enhance one another. Social sciences and hard sciences do not have to be seen as opposing worlds; they are both equally important to understanding the human condition and all of its intricate parts. Anthropology has understood that since the beginning of the twentieth century. And this is one of the things that makes it so invaluable.

126

✦ 6 ✦

Future Frontiers

AS WE COME TO THE END OF OUR BRIEF INTRODUCTION to anthropology as a whole, it is important to do more than simply look back at what the field has already done. Indeed, what should excite us most about anthropology (and indeed, any science) is what it has yet to do moving forward into the future.

One of the most recent and exciting developments in the realm of holistic, multiple-field approaches to understanding the world is the postulation of something called the **Anthropocene**. Anthropologists, ecologists, biologists, and others have collectively come together to vouch for the legitimacy of this concept. In short, the Anthropocene is a proposed categorization for the current time we live in in which human activity directly effects and irreversibly alters nature and the environment by simply existing in the capacity that we do. When we build, hunt, manufacture, travel, release greenhouse gasses, and so forth, we are bucking our nature and doing things that we were not built to do at the outset of our early human existence. At the time, nature accounted for our existence just like any other species of animal. But now that we have decided to harness nature for our use and dwell within it in capacities that alter it significantly, that is something that all of us scholars who study anything to do with the environment must account for. That includes anthropologists.

To demonstrate what this looks like in applied practice from an anthropological perspective, we can look at a couple of fairly recent examples. First up, a book by anthropologist Anna Lowenhaupt Tsing

called *The Mushroom at the End of the World*. In this book, a logging practice is shown to artificially reduce the number of a nearby growing mushroom known as the matsutake mushroom, effectively upping its rarity and subsequent value. As a result of this, the mushroom is considered a delicacy and sells for insane amounts of money as an import. Without that human activity altering the otherwise plentiful growth of this plant, the resulting market infatuation with and surrounding it would not have occurred. This not only affects nature itself, but other aspects of human society as well. Tsing's overarching argument is that, like the complexity of the various species of mushroom, humanity itself is

Future Frontiers

complexly intertwined with itself and other species on the planet, and that complexity, density, and chaotic beauty that eludes perfect categorization should be embraced and celebrated.

Another anthropologist interested in the much broader and far-reaching complex relationships between humans and nature is Eduardo Kohn, who wrote 2013's *How Forests Think: Toward an Anthropology Beyond the Human* over the course of a several-years-long ethnographic fieldwork studying and living among the Runa of Ecuador's Upper Amazon. There, while studying the complexity of that region and the native people's relation to it, Kohn realized that the conventional toolkit for ethnographic fieldwork fell short of giving him all the data he wished to have regarding the dynamics of how the Runa's interaction with nature affected and altered the ecosystem. As a result, he proposed new tools to add to the anthropological arsenal that incorporate elements from ecology and other environmental sciences. At one point in the book, Kohn illustrates the sheer weirdness of human presence altering the rhythm of nature by describing how a local pack of wild animals have developed an unspoken agreement with local villagers to share each other's hunting spoils and not attack each other. He also writes about what he describes as a "living sign" in which the Saussurian concept of the sign is amended and refined in the face of "semiosis," a more organic process in which one thought naturally gives rise to another, and that one then gives rise to yet another, and on it goes, all the while creating new sign concepts to things being experienced and altered in real-time in nature.

Collectively, these various approaches to embracing a more holistic and inter-dependent view of anthropological inquiry amounts to perhaps the biggest turn in the field since the scientific turn of Boas—this one an ontological turn of many voices aiming at the same connected and unified understanding of the world and the species that collectively affects it.

Many other modern anthropologists are finding more and more

ANTHROPOLOGY FOR BEGINNERS

ways to study and pull insight from the ways in which human beings are complexly intertwined with (and playing a role in the direction of) nature itself. But what about any other future frontiers for anthropologists to find relevant inquiries in? There's nature as a whole, a very widespread and epically proportioned frontier, to be sure. But there is also something quite contained and isolated that is peeking anthropological interests: the human brain.

Enter Daniel Lende and Greg Downy, the arguable spearheads of an emergent new potential subfield of anthropology being called neuroanthropology. Remember from the previous chapter the argument that if more fields of related inquiry on the human condition simply had more conversations with one another that more and more patches of ignorance and miscommunication would be filled in. This is the embodiment of that notion carried to its most logical conclusion. In neuroanthropology, all the richness of anthropology's subfields brings in yet another field to mingle and exchange data with: neuroscience.

This is important, because as more and more research on the brain is done, we discover just how culturally formed it truly is. The human

Future Frontiers

brain is plastic, meaning that it can physically be molded based on social interactions that the person who owns said brain takes part in. The latest studies on the frontier of the plastic brain suggests that everything from a person's gender characteristics to his ability to take standardized tests is at least in part informed by the brain being molded through social interaction.

The work of scholars like Cordelia Fine with her book *Delusions of Gender* and Victoria Pitts-Taylor with her book *The Brain's Body* takes highly scientific and empirical studies on the brain as a plastic organ that is informed in part by culture and draws very interesting social implications from said findings. Should we or should we not impose gendered expectations upon our children based on what sex they are born as? Is academic ability truly something that is hard-wired, or is that something affected by a person's socio-economic status and the stresses and social stigmas that come along with that? These are questions worth asking, and bringing together brain sciences and anthropology is an obvious next step in making those conversations happen where these fields relevantly cross and draw social implications.

Back to Downey and Lende, this is largely the point of their 2012 book *The Encultured Brain*: there are incredible benefits from merging these two fields and studying just how encultured the brain truly is and what that means for everything from interpersonal interaction on the one-on-one level to policy-making decisions in the future regarding sexuality or education. Without these empirical bulwarks firmly laid and delineated, the raw data on its own has no compass to find shore with. The social realities that are affected by findings like these are not to be taken lightly, and once again, anthropology seems incredibly well-equipped to take on said findings and find meaning in them—in both the lab and the living room.

Wherever anthropology goes next, it now has a unique and secure grounding in both empiricism and human empathy simultaneously, and it houses scholars who are excited to face the next big problem with both qualities proudly at the ready in their ever-growing arsenal of research tools. It truly is a grand time to be part of such a rich field, and the process of what will come next should excite anyone who has ever had the curiosity to muse to themselves, "I wonder where that came from."

GLOSSARY

absolute dating: methods of determining exact ages of unearthed artifacts and materials.

archaeology: the sub-field of anthropology concerned with uncovering buried artifacts from past human cultures.

biological anthropology: the sub-field of anthropology concerned with studying human anatomy, biology, and physical evolution.

cultural relativism: the perspective that each culture's values and practices should be understood (not necessarily condoned) based on its own context rather than be judged against the criteria of another culture's standards of normalcy. Not to be confused with moral relativism.

diaspora: the dispersion (or culture of merged dispersions) of a given group of people from their homeland.

ethnocentrism: the pseudoscientific perspective that all cultures should be judged based on the social and cultural norms of one's own society.

ethnography: the empirical practice of using participant observation processes over years within a given group of people to properly contextualize their culture and social practices.

ethnology: the academic process of comparing and contrasting various pieces of ethnographic data.

ANTHROPOLOGY FOR BEGINNERS

evolution: change through inheritable traits of biological populations over many generations.

functionalism: an approach of studying humanity that puts emphasis on individual aspects of human culture and society and delineates their purpose and interrelation through organic metaphor.

hypothesis: a proposed possible explanation of observed natural facts based on limited evidence; used as a starting point for scientific inquiry and rigorously tested.

liminal states: a social and cultural transitional state that is itself its own observable realty; betwixt and between more sustained social states of being. First observed by folklorist Arnold van Gennep but further developed in anthropological theory by sociocultural anthropologist Victor Turner.

linguistic anthropology: the sub-field of anthropology concerned with studying the evolution of language and its relationship to culture.

mores: social norms; expected conventions of a given culture or tradition.

natural selection: the process by which evolutionary processes are influenced by environmental need for a given species' survival.

performativity: the use of socially influenced behaviors as a means of outwardly expressing one's sense of identity and place.

phenotype: the trait that shows. Surface-level, observable characteristics or traits of organic individuals, such as morphology, development, etc. In humans, this predominantly appears through variations of skin tone, hair growth patterns, eyelid fat content, and so forth. Caused by environmental factors and not influenced by fundamental genetic differences. Visible but benign.

GLOSSARY

radiocarbon dating: an absolute dating process by which the degradation of Carbon-14 back into nitrogen is measured in organic materials to determine their age.

relative dating: methods of determining ages of unearthed artifacts and materials relative to absolutely dated adjacent finds.

the scientific method: the process of natural inquiry consisting of systematic observation, measurement, and experiment to propose and test hypotheses and build scientific theories.

the sign: comprised of two parts of language: the sound image (the signifier) and the concept/thing itself being identified (the signified). Related to process of encultured language formation as identified by Ferdinand de Saussure.

social Darwinism: the false belief that only the "fittest" among a biological group survive, and that natural selection rewards superior strength/intellect/other innate abilities rather than simply acts upon happenstance.

social facts: cultural norms that inform the behavior, internalized perceptions, and modes of control of a given society's inhabitants. Coined by Emile Durkheim.

sociocultural anthropology: the sub-field of anthropology concerned with examining human culture.

structuralism: an approach of studying humanity from a perspective in which all individual elements are understood as merely parts of larger, overarching wholes.

unilinear evolutionism: the pseudoscientific "theory" peddled by social Darwinists that distinct human groups evolve in a linear fashion from primitive to advanced separate from each other.

FURTHER READING

Charles Darwin, *The Voyage of the Beagle*. Washington, DC: National Geographic Adventure Classics, 2004; Orig. Ed. 1839.

Charles Darwin, *On the Origin of Species*. London: Penguin Classics, 2009; Orig. Ed. 1859.

Charles Darwin, *The Descent of Man*. London: Penguin Classics, 2004; Orig. Ed. 1871.

Ian Tattersall, *The Fossil Trail: How We Know What We Think We Know About Human Evolution*. Oxford: Oxford University Press, 2008.

Jerry A. Coyne, *Why Evolution is True*. London: Penguin Books, 2010.

Robert Wald Sussman, *The Myth of Race: The Troubling Persistence of an Unscientific Idea*. Cambridge: Harvard University Press, 2016.

Ferdinand de Saussure, *Course in General Linguistics*. Illinois: Open Court, 1998; Orig. Ed. 1916.

Noam Chomsky & Robert C. Berwick, *Why Only Us: Language and Evolution*. Cambridge: The MIT Press, 2017.

Marcel Mauss, *The Gift*. New York: W.W. Norton, 1990; Orig. Ed. 1925.

Mary Douglass, *Purity and Danger: An Analysis of the Concepts of Pollution and Taboo*. London, New York: Routledge, 1991; Orig. Ed. 1966.

Zora Neale Hurston, *Mules and Men*. New York: Harper, 2008.

ANTHROPOLOGY FOR BEGINNERS

Alan Barnard, *History and Theory in Anthropology*. Cambridge: Cambridge University Press, 2000.

Victor Turner, *The Forest of Symbols*. Ithaca: Cornell University Press, 1970; Orig. Ed. 1967

Victor Turner, *The Ritual Process*. London, New York: Routledge, 1996; Orig. Ed. 1969

Kath Weston, *Families We Choose*. New York: Columbia University Press, 1997.

Daniel H. Lende & Greg Downey, *The Encultured Brain: An Introduction to Neuroanthropology*. Cambridge: The MIT Press, 2015.

Eduardo Kohn, *How Forests Think: Toward an Anthropology Beyond the Human*. Berkeley: University of California Press, 2013.

About the Author

MICAH J. FLECK received his degree in anthropology from Columbia University. He is a writer, editor, and researcher who has appeared in various publications as well as on public television discussing topics such as education, the learning brain, gender, and the anthropology of political populism.

About the Illustrator

LUCA F. CAREY lives in the Bronx and paints pictures of monsters and beautiful horrific visions from other dimensions. He is an alumnus of the Savannah College of Art and Design and is currently working multiple niche projects.

THE FOR BEGINNERS® SERIES

ABSTRACT EXPRESSIONISM	ISBN 978-1-939994-62-2
AFRICAN HISTORY FOR BEGINNERS	ISBN 978-1-934389-18-8
AMERICAN PRESIDENCY, THE	ISBN 978-1-939994-70-7
ANARCHISM FOR BEGINNERS	ISBN 978-1-934389-32-4
ARABS & ISRAEL FOR BEGINNERS	ISBN 978-1-934389-16-4
ART THEORY FOR BEGINNERS	ISBN 978-1-934389-47-8
ASTRONOMY FOR BEGINNERS	ISBN 978-1-934389-25-6
AYN RAND FOR BEGINNERS	ISBN 978-1-934389-37-9
BARACK OBAMA FOR BEGINNERS, AN ESSENTIAL GUIDE	ISBN 978-1-934389-44-7
BEN FRANKLIN FOR BEGINNERS	ISBN 978-1-934389-48-5
BLACK HISTORY FOR BEGINNERS	ISBN 978-1-934389-19-5
THE BLACK HOLOCAUST FOR BEGINNERS	ISBN 978-1-934389-03-4
BLACK PANTHERS FOR BEGINNERS	ISBN 978-1-939994-39-4
BLACK WOMEN FOR BEGINNERS	ISBN 978-1-934389-20-1
BUDDHA FOR BEGINNERS	ISBN 978-1-939994-33-2
BUKOWSKI FOR BEGINNERS	ISBN 978-1-939994-37-0
CHICANO MOVEMENT FOR BEGINNERS	ISBN 978-1-939994-64-6
CHOMSKY FOR BEGINNERS	ISBN 978-1-934389-17-1
CIVIL RIGHTS FOR BEGINNERS	ISBN 978-1-934389-89-8
CLIMATE CHANGE FOR BEGINNERS	ISBN 978-1-939994-43-1
DADA & SURREALISM FOR BEGINNERS	ISBN 978-1-934389-00-3
DANTE FOR BEGINNERS	ISBN 978-1-934389-67-6
DECONSTRUCTION FOR BEGINNERS	ISBN 978-1-934389-26-3
DEMOCRACY FOR BEGINNERS	ISBN 978-1-934389-36-2
DERRIDA FOR BEGINNERS	ISBN 978-1-934389-11-9
EASTERN PHILOSOPHY FOR BEGINNERS	ISBN 978-1-934389-07-2
EXISTENTIALISM FOR BEGINNERS	ISBN 978-1-934389-21-8
FANON FOR BEGINNERS	ISBN 978-1-934389-87-4
FDR AND THE NEW DEAL FOR BEGINNERS	ISBN 978-1-934389-50-8
FIRST AMENDMENT	ISBN 978-1-939994-74-5
FOUCAULT FOR BEGINNERS	ISBN 978-1-934389-12-6
FREEMASONRY FOR BEGINNERS	ISBN 978-1-939994-56-1
FRENCH REVOLUTIONS FOR BEGINNERS	ISBN 978-1-934389-91-1
GENDER & SEXUALITY FOR BEGINNERS	ISBN 978-1-934389-69-0
GREEK MYTHOLOGY FOR BEGINNERS	ISBN 978-1-934389-83-6
HARRIET TUBMAN FOR BEGINNERS	ISBN 978-1-939994-72-1
HEIDEGGER FOR BEGINNERS	ISBN 978-1-934389-13-3

www.forbeginnersbooks.com

THE FOR BEGINNERS® SERIES

THE HISTORY OF CLASSICAL MUSIC FOR BEGINNERS	ISBN 978-1-939994-26-4
THE HISTORY OF OPERA FOR BEGINNERS	ISBN 978-1-934389-79-9
ISLAM FOR BEGINNERS	ISBN 978-1-934389-01-0
JANE AUSTEN FOR BEGINNERS	ISBN 978-1-934389-61-4
JUNG FOR BEGINNERS	ISBN 978-1-934389-76-8
KIERKEGAARD FOR BEGINNERS	ISBN 978-1-934389-14-0
LACAN FOR BEGINNERS	ISBN 978-1-934389-39-3
LIBERTARIANISM FOR BEGINNERS	ISBN 978-1-939994-66-0
LINCOLN FOR BEGINNERS	ISBN 978-1-934389-85-0
LINGUISTICS FOR BEGINNERS	ISBN 978-1-934389-28-7
LITERARY THEORY FOR BEGINNERS	ISBN 978-1-939994-60-8
MALCOLM X FOR BEGINNERS	ISBN 978-1-934389-04-1
MARX'S DAS KAPITAL FOR BEGINNERS	ISBN 978-1-934389-59-1
MCLUHAN FOR BEGINNERS	ISBN 978-1-934389-75-1
MORMONISM FOR BEGINNERS	ISBN 978-1-939994-52-3
MUSIC THEORY FOR BEGINNERS	ISBN 978-1-939994-46-2
NIETZSCHE FOR BEGINNERS	ISBN 978-1-934389-05-8
PAUL ROBESON FOR BEGINNERS	ISBN 978-1-934389-81-2
PHILOSOPHY FOR BEGINNERS	ISBN 978-1-934389-02-7
PLATO FOR BEGINNERS	ISBN 978-1-934389-08-9
POETRY FOR BEGINNERS	ISBN 978-1-934389-46-1
POSTMODERNISM FOR BEGINNERS	ISBN 978-1-934389-09-6
PRISON INDUSTRIAL COMPLEX FOR BEGINNERS	ISBN 978-1-939994-31-8
PROUST FOR BEGINNERS	ISBN 978-1-939994-44-8
RELATIVITY & QUANTUM PHYSICS FOR BEGINNERS	ISBN 978-1-934389-42-3
SARTRE FOR BEGINNERS	ISBN 978-1-934389-15-7
SAUSSURE FOR BEGINNERS	ISBN 978-1-939994-41-7
SHAKESPEARE FOR BEGINNERS	ISBN 978-1-934389-29-4
STANISLAVSKI FOR BEGINNERS	ISBN 978-1-939994-35-6
STRUCTURALISM & POSTSTRUCTURALISM FOR BEGINNERS	ISBN 978-1-934389-10-2
TESLA FOR BEGINNERS	ISBN 978-1-939994-48-6
TONI MORRISON FOR BEGINNERS	ISBN 978-1-939994-54-7
WOMEN'S HISTORY FOR BEGINNERS	ISBN 978-1-934389-60-7
UNIONS FOR BEGINNERS	ISBN 978-1-934389-77-5
U.S. CONSTITUTION FOR BEGINNERS	ISBN 978-1-934389-62-1
ZEN FOR BEGINNERS	ISBN 978-1-934389-06-5
ZINN FOR BEGINNERS	ISBN 978-1-934389-40-9

www.forbeginnersbooks.com